INSIDE THE AMERICAN LEGAL MIND

Inside the American Legal Mind: An International Practitioner Guide to American Legal Reasoning clearly explains how to navigate within U.S. legal practice. A combination of common law legal history with the straight-shooting American style has resulted in an approach to issue analysis that is structurally different from other fields and from the civil law systems common in other countries. Precedent drives the interpretive process, providing the pillars upon which an American lawyer builds a case. Understanding how to capture relevant aspects of precedent, merge those aspects with precedent from seemingly distinct cases, and apply the resulting formula to a given fact pattern can be a harrowing experience for anyone untrained in American legal thinking.

This book bridges that gap for aspiring lawyers in America as well as for foreign legal practitioners. Fandl clearly and concisely demonstrates how to research, analyze, and ultimately condense legal ideas into written form in the American legal style. Suitable for undergraduates in U.S. Criminal Justice programs and for LL.M. courses, as well as for continuing education for professionals.

Kevin J. Fandl is a Professor of Legal Studies and Global Business Strategy at the Fox School of Business at Temple University. He had previously served as Chief of Staff for international trade and intellectual property at U.S. Immigration and Customs Enforcement. In 2011, he founded the Global Legal Education Institute, which delivers intensive practical law courses to foreign legal practitioners and advanced law students around the world.

Kevin Fandl's *Inside the American Legal Mind: An International Practitioner Guide to American Legal Reasoning* guides readers through a quick but thorough outline of the American legal environment, its differences, its eccentricities, and the minds at work within it. Accessible to both students and professionals alike, *Inside the American Legal Mind* incorporates case law, analysis, and astute observations about the origins and precedent of the American legal system and its practitioners. It is a valuable resource to all those interested in grasping better hold of the nuanced world of American jurisprudence.

Kim C. Phan, International Law Institute

Years ago when I first started law teaching I taught a course on the introduction to U.S. law to foreign lawyers at the Harvard Law School's International Tax Program. At that time I hoped someone would produce a comprehensive text to be used in such a course. Kevin Fandl's new work *Inside the American Legal Mind* now fulfills that hope. This is an excellent work.

Stuart S. Malawer, J.D., Ph.D., George Mason University

The content of this book goes right to the point of what students need: how to find, understand, organize and convey the information in a legal context. While other books address these issues, they also cover other topics of common interest for international students. This outline is more fine-tuned to achieve a successful understanding of legal reasoning.

Carlos Ivan Davila, Georgetown University

Kevin Fandl is an author whose work can bridge countries and cultures. By delving into the "American Legal Mind," this new book will provide international practitioners with a deeper understanding and appreciation of U.S. legal practice, procedure, reasoning, and results.

Prof. Mark E. Wojcik, The John Marshall Law School

eRESOURCES

A range of further resources for this book is available at www.routledge.com/9780323356473

INSIDE THE AMERICAN LEGAL MIND

An International Practitioner Guide to American Legal Reasoning

Kevin J. Fandl

Routledge
Taylor & Francis Group
NEW YORK AND LONDON

First published 2016
by Routledge
711 Third Avenue, New York, NY 10017

and by Routledge
2 Park Square, Milton Park, Abingdon, Oxon OX14 4RN

Routledge is an imprint of the Taylor & Francis Group, an informa business

Library of Congress Cataloging-in-Publication Data
Fandl, Kevin J.
Understanding the American legal mind : a practical guide / Kevin J. Fandl.
pages cm
Includes bibliographical references and index.
1. Practice of law—United States. 2. Law—United States. 3. Law—United States—Methodology. I. Title.
KF300.F36 2015
349.73—dc23
2015013662

ISBN: 978-1-138-93781-9 (hbk)
ISBN: 978-0-323-35647-3 (pbk)
ISBN: 978-1-315-63803-4 (ebk)

Typeset in New Baskerville
by Apex CoVantage, LLC

CONTENTS

INTRODUCTION

Over the last ten years, I have had the opportunity to train thousands of legal and business professionals around the world on the nuances of the U.S. legal system. I have worked with law firms, chambers of commerce, international organizations, and universities, responding to their requests for a better understanding of how law works in the United States. Many of the participants in my trainings have clients that do business in the United States, while some others are interested in eventually practicing there. In all cases, my seminar participants are eager to know how common law lawyers think, work, and write.

In the beginning, I tried to teach professionals abroad and foreign professionals in the United States the same way that I had taught American law students. I assigned cases to read, directed students to appropriate statutes, and gave lectures about key principles in the U.S. legal system from contracts to torts to civil procedure. But I quickly realized that my approach with foreign and non-law practitioners was not garnering the same results that I was accustomed to with my American students. I knew that it was not for a lack of legal knowledge; in fact, most of the foreign legal professionals impressed me immensely with their knowledge of legal concepts in their country and in the United States. So what was the reason that I was not breaking through and seeing the results I expected?

I began examining the legal education system in some of the civil law countries where I regularly lectured to try to discern the differences in education that might account for the differences in outcomes that I was seeing. In many of these countries, law students are educated principally through a doctrinal approach that places the professor as the expert and the student as the recipient of knowledge that they are expected to recall. The professor *informs* the students about what the law is and the student memorizes innumerable statutes, regulations, and decrees to develop their competence. Testing is often a series of oral examinations whereby students are asked to recite provisions from statutes that they were taught.

The legal education approach in the United States is quite distinct. In an American classroom, professors are certainly respected as highly knowledgeable, but they are not placed on pedestals as *givers* of knowledge. Rather, their role is to awaken the minds of the students by challenging their interpretations of the law and forcing them to think about issues in unique ways. Students, similarly, are not *recipients* of knowledge but rather active participants in the learning process. They are expected to challenge concepts presented by their professors and their colleagues; they are expected to raise questions about cases they read; and they are expected to be highly critical of everything they read. Examinations are usually written hypothetical fact patterns to which students must use their critical thinking and analysis skills to resolve complex legal questions. The goal of the American-style legal education system is not to develop cadres of legal experts replete with memorized legal concepts; rather, it is to develop critical thinkers that are prepared to stretch their minds to address novel issues or to resolve complex issues in novel ways.

The civil and common law legal education systems are both producing the types of lawyers that they need to work within their own legal systems. Civil law lawyers must be well-versed in applicable statutes and must be capable of reciting them correctly and applying them to their cases. Common law lawyers are expected to have broad knowledge of many cases as well as the ability to extract salient points from those cases to develop coherent arguments for their clients. Accordingly, the legal education systems are working to produce lawyers with appropriate skills.

However, the traditional approach to learning the law that is taught in both of these jurisdictions is not producing enough lawyers capable of successful global practice. Today's global business environment means that more and more legal guidance is cutting across national borders. Firms of all sizes are capitalizing on the ability to operate in multiple jurisdictions, and they require legal guidance for their contracts and other commercial actions. The United States is a major market for many of these firms, meaning that it is only a matter of time before a civil law jurisdiction firm will require advice about working with partners or outposts in common law jurisdictions. The lawyers of today must be trained to provide the guidance that their global clients of the future will need.

This book is not a call for a revolution in legal education. Instead, it is a small step in helping civil law practitioners prepare for work in a common law legal environment. The best preparation for such practitioners would be to relocate to the United States and pursue a Juris Doctor degree in law at an American law school, where they will spend their first year learning the art of legal reasoning and analysis. But this requires an extensive investment of time and money, which most busy practitioners are unwilling to make. Accordingly, this book serves as practitioner's fast track to understanding the American legal mind from the point of view of a practitioner, rather than a fresh law student.

In the following pages, you will find the same concepts that you might see in a first-year American law course on legal reasoning, with one important caveat—I am making the presumption that you have already been trained in the law of your own jurisdiction. A first-year law student in the United States would not generally know the elements of a valid contract, the meaning of civil procedure, or the role of arbitration in resolving business disputes. I presume that you already know these things, at least to a basic degree. This presumption allows me to move quickly into the development of key legal reasoning skills.

You will note that a large portion of this book consists of case law excerpts. As I explain in the common law history chapter (Chapter 2), this is because law in the United States is primarily developed through the rulings of courts. Though our legislature is by no means inactive in promulgating statutes, it is our courts that ultimately review those statutes and interpret their meaning. This means that our legal reasoning emanates directly from the legal reasoning of the courts. This is why I have chosen to present you with many case examples to help you understand how an American lawyer thinks.

I hope this book is a first step in your pathway toward a global legal practice that includes work in the United States. The business environment today has forged a borderless world in many ways, engaging in joint ventures, export operations, franchises, and other multi-jurisdictional relationships. It is time for the legal profession to catch up and provide the legal guidance that they no doubt require.

Kevin J. Fandl
Washington, D.C., March 5, 2015

1

THE VALUE IN UNDERSTANDING AMERICAN LEGAL REASONING

Take the following scenario and try to express the legal issue that you see:

Susan Powers, your client, has a five-year supply contract with Gordon Lewis, whereby she will provide avocados to Mr. Lewis for his small Mexican restaurant. The contract does not specify a minimum or maximum order quantity, but Mr. Lewis generally orders 100 kilos of avocados per month. However, last month, he ordered only 20 kilos of avocados, claiming that a sushi restaurant opened next door and has taken away many of his customers. Ms. Powers believes this to be unacceptable as she counted on the income from the 100-avocado orders that Mr. Lewis had been placing. She would like to sue for breach of contract.

This is a simple commercial contract case, and I have left out many details, such as where the parties are located, to keep it simple. Based on what you have read and what you know about law in your country, what do you see as the principal issue that you need to help Ms. Powers with? You may have realized that this is a requirements contract, which does not specify an actual quantity but only provides an estimate of anticipated need. Parties to this type of contract can adjust their quantities as needed so long as those adjustments are reasonable. So it seems that we can argue that Mr. Lewis's downward adjustment in quantity was unreasonable. But how do you know for sure?

In your country, you may have the ability to look to a commercial code. That code might tell you what is considered reasonable in open quantity contracts like this, and from there you could extract the guidance that you need for your client. You will be well positioned to advise Ms. Powers and relatively confident in how the courts will handle this issue in your country.

Let's now assume that this is a case taking place entirely within the United States. The issue is the same—did Mr. Lewis breach his contract with Ms. Powers by substantially reducing the quantity ordered? You may look for a code to help you answer this question, and you would be in luck. The Uniform Commercial Code (UCC) governs commercial contracts like this and will provide you some valuable guidance. In this case, we can look to section 2–306(1) of the UCC, which says:

> *A term which measures the quantity by the output of the* seller *or the requirements of the* buyer *means such actual output or requirements as may occur in* good faith, *except that no quantity unreasonably disproportionate to any stated estimate or in the absence of a stated estimate to any normal or otherwise comparable prior output or requirements may be tendered or demanded.*

Great, problem solved, right? The code seems fairly clear in stating that a party cannot request an unreasonable change in quantity when no quantity is specified in the contract. So we can advise Ms. Powers that we believe this was unreasonable and she has a winning case—can't we? Unlike in civil law countries, the Code is only the starting point. The ultimate decision rests with the courts, and the courts are responsible for interpreting the code. So no matter what the code says, you must also look to cases to develop your guidance to the client.

Using a variety of search tools, which we will discuss later in this book, we can look for cases that interpret UCC § 2–306(1). The good news is that our search will yield roughly 2,000 cases that address this issue in some way. Of course, that is also the bad news. How do we select the "right" case? Let's say that we go with one of the first cases in the list, a case from New York, because it seems to speak directly to our issue. In that case, the judge said:

> *Courts are split on the question whether the "unreasonably disproportionate" provision applies only to disproportionate increases in demand. On its face, the text of the statute appears to apply to both increases and decreases. The commentary to the section is unhelpful and ambiguous. On the one hand, section 2 of the commentary indicates that "good faith variations from prior requirements are permitted even when the variation may be such as to result in discontinuance," providing support for the idea that the statute applies only to disproportionate increases. On the other hand, section 3 states that "the agreed estimate is to be regarded as a center around which the parties intend the variation to occur," clearly contemplating variation in both directions.*
>
> *I agree with the reasoning of the majority of courts and commentators, who have concluded that the "unreasonably disproportionate" provision does not apply to cases of decreased demand.*[1]

The language of the court is surprisingly clear. This judge seems emphatic in rejecting the use of § 2–306 to terminate a requirements contract when the other party *reduces* demand. You should also note that the judge makes clear the fact that the Code itself does not answer this question, so it is up to him, as a member of the judicial branch, to make this decision.

Now, with both the Code and this case in hand, are we ready to provide advice to Ms. Powers? What would that advice be at this stage? Right now, it appears clear that Mr. Lewis did not act wrongfully in reducing his demand under a requirements contract. But we can't provide this guidance to Ms. Powers just yet.

The United States is not only a common law country; it is also a federalist country, meaning that it consists of numerous state governments and a single federal government, all of which maintain their own courts. As I will explain later, federalism means that the decisions of state courts and state legislatures have geographical limits. This means that decisions from one state will not necessarily carry any weight in another state. Because of that, it is essential that we know not only where our parties are litigating or arbitrating their case, but which cases and statutes we are using to guide them through that process.

The decision of the court above is from a federal court located in the Eastern District of New York. That is a very small judicial district that covers Brooklyn, New York. So if our contract is being litigated in Brooklyn, we may need to pay close attention to this opinion, even though it is from a federal court and most contracts cases are resolved in state courts. If we are anywhere other than Brooklyn, the language from the court above becomes "persuasive," meaning that our judge doesn't need to follow that guidance.

What you are hopefully beginning to see is that Ms. Powers's issue, while simple on its face, requires a great deal of care in its analysis and resolution. What you saw above were the procedural issues that have to be taken into account when starting off down the road of legal research. And while we will discuss those in this book, the principal focus will not be in finding cases, but rather in understanding how to use them to your advantage.

Legal analysis is the logical process of extracting ideas from numerous legal authorities to form legal opinions. It is an entirely new way of thinking for most people and requires the ability to associate (or disassociate) often conflicting reasoning and diverse fact patterns in order to formulate a single convincing idea. Unlike in other social sciences, which start from a single theory and develop multiple applications for that theory, legal analysis means taking multiple applications of an idea and extracting a single theory from those applications.

Civil law lawyers are taught law within the social sciences much like philosophy or economics. Law emanates from the legislative bodies in these countries and is often quite extensive and detailed in its explanations. Courts in these countries, though they no doubt have the flexibility to interpret this law, do so on a case-by-case basis, never establishing a new meaning for the law that modifies what the legislature has said. Accordingly, law is taught as the memorization of these extensive statutes, rather than a survey of how they have been applied across different courts. A civil law lawyer becomes an expert in expressing what the law is and applying it to a variety of situations. A common law lawyer becomes an expert in understanding a multitude of interpretations of the law and can use legal analysis skills to resolve a single case.

No method is better or worse than the other. Civil law countries have many advantages, such as predictability and consistency in the law. Rarely is a civil law lawyer surprised at the outcome of a single case (though they may be surprised at the outcome of a legislative session). Common law countries have their own advantages, such as flexibility and adaptability in the law. There are many "bad" decisions made by both legislators and judges in common law countries; but a common law lawyer is always ready with an argument to convince a judge to reject past decisions in favor of creating new precedent.

Legal Reasoning as an Evolution of Ideas

Let's take a recent example—same-sex marriage. The U.S. Congress made efforts to prevent same-sex couples from marrying and receiving benefits under the law, such as the right to inherit from a deceased spouse without paying taxes on a substantial portion of the inheritance. President Bill Clinton set forth the policy and the Congress ultimately passed the Defense of Marriage Act in 1996 (DOMA).[2] That Act limits the federal definition of "marriage" to only heterosexual couples. Section 3 of the Act states the following:

> *In determining the meaning of any Act of Congress, or of any ruling, regulation, or interpretation of the various administrative bureaus and agencies of the United States, the word 'marriage' means only a legal union between one man and one woman as husband and wife, and the word 'spouse' refers only to a person of the opposite sex who is a husband or a wife.*

However, as a federalist system, this federal statute only applied to federal benefits. The Constitution did not give the federal government the authority to regulate marriage, which means that such power rests with the states.[3] In fact, section 2 of DOMA makes that clear:

> *No State, territory, or possession of the United States, or Indian tribe, shall be required to give effect to any public act, record, or judicial proceeding of any other State, territory, possession, or tribe respecting a relationship between persons of the same sex that is treated as a marriage under the laws of such other State, territory, possession, or tribe, or a right or claim arising from such relationship.*

Though the language appears to encourage states to outlaw same-sex marriage, the language is in effect preserving the rights of the states to choose how they wish to legislate in this area. States took heed and many passed state statutes outlawing same-sex marriage, while others expressly offered legal benefits to same-sex couples. Since the federal government could not force the states to act without amending the Constitution (a very difficult process), the right of same-sex marriage varied depending on which state you lived in.

DOMA was challenged in 2010 by Edie Windsor, a Russian immigrant born in Philadelphia who married Thea Clara Spyer in Canada, where same-sex marriage was legal. The couple lived in New York (which legalized same-sex marriage in 2011). Spyer died in 2009 and left a substantial inheritance for her same-sex spouse. However, as there is no protection under federal law for passing inheritances to unmarried partners, Windsor was levied $363,053 in taxes on the "gift" from her deceased spouse. She sued to challenge section 3 of DOMA.

The case was ultimately decided by the U.S. Supreme Court, which decided in 2012 that section 3 of DOMA was unconstitutional. In its role as the interpreter of both laws and the Constitution, its decision served as the final word on the matter.[4] This meant that Windsor would not be subjected to the tax and also that the federal statute, at least section 3, is no longer valid.

The decision did not change the state of affairs for state courts. Even though *Windsor* definitively legalized same-sex marriage at the federal level, nothing was said about whether states had to follow suit. In his dissent from the *Windsor* majority, conservative Justice Antonin Scalia predicted that the majority's decision was the beginning of the end for all bans on same-sex marriage. "No one should be fooled; it is just a matter of listening and waiting for the other shoe," he said.

The *Windsor* decision gave same-sex marriage advocates precedent from the highest court in the United States to attack the constitutionality of state bans on same-sex marriage. Four intermediate federal appellate courts (Fourth, Seventh, Ninth, and Tenth) and numerous federal district courts have already ruled that such bans are unconstitutional. By striking down the bans, these courts effectively overruled the legislatures in the states over which they have jurisdiction. As of the time of this writing, 32 states either had their bans overruled or proactively authorized same-sex marriage.

However, in 2014, the Sixth Circuit Court of Appeals, which includes Kentucky, Michigan, Ohio, and Tennessee, upheld state bans on same-sex marriage, going against the trend of other federal intermediate appellate courts. The only court above the federal intermediate appellate courts is the U.S. Supreme Court, and this "split" creates uncertainty in the correct interpretation of the law. Consider the opinion of the Sixth Circuit Court:

> *Through a mixture of common law decisions, statutes, and constitutional provisions, each State in the Sixth Circuit has long adhered to the traditional definition of marriage.*[5]
>
> *In trying to figure out the original meaning of a provision, it is fair to say, the line between interpretation and evolution blurs from time to time. That is an occupational hazard for judges when it comes to old or generally worded provisions. Yet that knotty problem does not confront us. Yes, the Fourteenth Amendment is old; the*

people ratified it in 1868. And yes, it is generally worded; it says: "[N]or shall any State deprive any person of life, liberty, or property, without due process of law; nor deny to any person within its jurisdiction the equal protection of the laws." Nobody in this case, however, argues that the people who adopted the Fourteenth Amendment understood it to require the States to change the definition of marriage.[6]

What we are left with is this: By creating a status (marriage) and by subsidizing it (e.g., with tax-filing privileges and deductions), the States created an incentive for two people who procreate together to stay together for purposes of rearing offspring. That does not convict the States of irrationality, only of awareness of the biological reality that couples of the same sex do not have children in the same way as couples of opposite sexes and that couples of the same sex do not run the risk of unintended offspring. That explanation, still relevant today, suffices to allow the States to retain authority over an issue they have regulated from the beginning.[7]

If all else fails, the plaintiffs invite us to consider that "[a] core strength of the American legal system . . . is its capacity to evolve" in response to new ways of thinking about old policies. DeBoer Appellees' Br. at 57–58. But even if we accept this invitation and put aside the past—original meaning, tradition, time-respected doctrine—that does not take the plaintiffs where they wish to go. We could, to be sure, look at this case alongside evolving moral and policy considerations. The Supreme Court has done so before. Lawrence, 539 U.S. at 573. It may do so again. "A prime part of the history of our Constitution . . . is the story of the extension of constitutional rights . . . to people once ignored or excluded." United States v. Virginia, 518 U.S. 515, 557 (1996). Why not do so here?[8]

When the courts do not let the people resolve new social issues like this one, they perpetuate the idea that the heroes in these change events are judges and lawyers. Better in this instance, we think, to allow change through the customary political processes, in which the people, gay and straight alike, become the heroes of their own stories by meeting each other not as adversaries in a court system but as fellow citizens seeking to resolve a new social issue in a fair-minded way.[9]

The court goes to extensive lengths to explain why it wants to leave the decision about same-sex marriage to the states. Its ruling is not suggesting that states cannot allow same-sex marriage; rather, the court is saying that the federal government lacks the power to prevent it from banning same-sex marriage at the state level. In essence, the plaintiffs in this case were attempting to use the precedent established in *Windsor*, combined with the decisions in several other federal courts, to establish a pseudo-Constitutional right to same-sex marriage. The majority of the Sixth Circuit was unwilling to go that far.

The dissent of Judge Martha Craig Daughtrey is worth noting:

> *These plaintiffs are not political zealots trying to push reform on their fellow citizens; they are committed same-sex couples, many of them heading up de facto families, who want to achieve equal status—de jure status, if you will—with their married neighbors, friends, and coworkers, to be accepted as contributing members of their social and religious communities, and to be welcomed as fully legitimate parents at their children's schools. They seek to do this by virtue of exercising a civil right that most of us take for granted—the right to marry.*
>
> *For although my colleagues in the majority pay lip service to marriage as an institution conceived for the purpose of providing a stable family unit "within which children may flourish," they ignore the destabilizing effect of its absence in the homes of tens of thousands of same-sex parents throughout the four states of the Sixth Circuit.*
>
> *Instead of recognizing the plaintiffs as persons, suffering actual harm as a result of being denied the right to marry where they reside or the right to have their valid marriages recognized there, my colleagues view the plaintiffs as social activists who have somehow stumbled into federal court.*[10]

It is worth noting that the Sixth Circuit Court of Appeals has a poor track record with the U.S. Supreme Court. Its rulings have been overturned by the high court in 24 of the last 25 decisions between 2008 and 2013.[11]

The Ninth Circuit opinion, the most recent federal intermediate appellate court opposing state bans on gay marriage as of this writing, asserts that it is the duty of the courts to prevent discrimination in the interest of preventing harm to minorities (same-sex couples in this case). They use *Windsor* as a starting point for cleansing the country of discriminatory state laws. Excerpts from that opinion follow:

> *Idaho and Nevada's marriage laws, by preventing same-sex couples from marrying and refusing to recognize same-sex marriages celebrated elsewhere, impose profound legal, financial, social and psychic harms on numerous citizens of those states. These harms are not inflicted on opposite-sex couples, who may, if they wish, enjoy the rights and assume the responsibilities of marriage. Laws that treat people differently based on sexual orientation are unconstitutional unless a "legitimate purpose . . . overcome[s]" the injury inflicted by the law on lesbians and gays and their families. SmithKline, 740 F.3d at 481–82.*[12]
>
> *Defendants' essential contention is that bans on same-sex marriage promote the welfare of children, by encouraging good parenting in stable opposite-sex families. Heightened scrutiny, however, demands more than speculation and conclusory assertions, especially when the assertions are of such little merit. Defendants have presented no evidence of any such effect. Indeed, they cannot even explain the manner in which, as they predict, children of opposite-sex couples will be harmed. Their other contentions are equally without merit. Because defendants have failed to demonstrate that these laws further any legitimate purpose, they unjustifiably discriminate on the basis of sexual orientation, and are in violation of the Equal Protection Clause.*[13]

The court then goes on to argue by analogy, a skill that we will develop later in this text:

> *The lessons of our constitutional history are clear: inclusion strengthens, rather than weakens, our most important institutions.*

> *When we integrated our schools, education improved. See Brown v. Bd. of Educ. of Topeka, 347 U.S. 483, 492–95 (1954). When we opened our juries to women, our democracy became more vital. See Taylor v. Louisiana, 419 U.S. 522, 535–37 (1975). When we allowed lesbian and gay soldiers to serve openly in uniform, it enhanced unit cohesion. See Witt v. Dep't of Air Force, 527 F.3d 806, 821 n.11 (9th Cir. 2008). When same-sex couples are married, just as when opposite-sex couples are married, they serve as models of loving commitment to all.*[14]

The unanimous court overruled the bans in Alaska, Arizona, and Montana, the states over which it has jurisdiction and in which such bans existed. This "split" in opinions places the U.S. Supreme Court in the precarious position of arbiter—if it chooses not to act upon an appeal from any of these Circuit Court decisions, courts will be left without effective guidance to address future same-sex marriage cases.

This discussion was not meant to highlight the importance of same-sex marriage as a legal debate; rather, it is meant to highlight the often radically different opinions of equally astute judges across high-level courts and the role of legal analysis in reaching their conclusions. The Sixth Circuit followed the logic of federalism, choosing to interpret existing precedent as only applicable in limited instances and not creating any broad power for the federal government. The Ninth Circuit used many of the same precedents to extrapolate a more active role for the federal courts in guiding the decisions of states in their promulgation of laws in this area. Both forms of analysis are persuasive and logical, regardless of which conclusion ultimately controls when the Supreme Court takes up the issue in the future.

Why You Should Study American Legal Reasoning Today

Same-sex marriage may not be one of the issues in your international client files. But regardless of the issue, understanding common law legal analysis is critical in managing a successful global law practice. More than ever before, law is crossing borders and making its way into venues facing many of these issues for the first time ever. Being prepared not just with the proper case law but also with the proper legal analysis will place a lawyer on solid footing in any courtroom, boardroom, or arbitral tribunal.

And where will that courtroom or tribunal be? Despite its many disadvantages, American courts are still the favored locus for resolving non-arbitral issues. Unlike many judicial systems, American courts offer a relatively low-cost, consistent, and transparent forum to resolve international disputes. Juries are often highlighted as the wild card in U.S. litigation; however, some types of trials, including many business disputes, never face a jury. And even those that do generally have the ability to appeal unfavorable verdicts that might have been based more on emotion than on the facts of the case.

Even with the reduced likelihood of facing a jury in an international business dispute in American courts, it is worth spending a few minutes explaining how the jury process works and the risks that it poses to foreign litigants. It may seem unusual to some that U.S. courts rely to a large degree on the opinions of twelve citizens who generally lack legal training and any particular skill at rooting out the facts in a case. Though the jurors can ask questions, they rarely do, making them different from the audience only in that they decide the fate of the defendant.

The Unpredictable Jury

The concept of trial by jury has its roots in medieval England, likely during the reign of King Henry III. Legal Scholar William Blackstone, writing in the 18th century, commented on the 17th century institutionalization of the jury as the finders of evidence in a trial. A jury provides a "strong and two–fold barrier . . . between the liberties of the people and the prerogative of the crown" because "the truth of every accusation. . . . [must] be confirmed by the unanimous suffrage of twelve of his equals and neighbors indifferently chosen and superior to all suspicion."[15] The second barrier for Blackstone was the grand jury, discussed below.

When British emigrants laid out the principles for the judiciary in the Constitution, they made certain that jury trials, by that time commonplace in England, would remain part of the American legal system. The right to a jury trial in both civil and criminal cases was adopted by the U.S. Constitution as well as by the constitutions of the original thirteen colonies. The Constitution also extended the right to all states in the case of criminal charges.

Juries in U.S. trials were established by our Constitution. Criminal cases in both state and federal courts require juries. This is established by the third Article of the U.S. Constitution:

> *Trial of all Crimes, except in Cases of Impeachment, shall be by Jury; and such Trial shall be held in the State where the said Crimes shall have been committed; but when not committed within any State, the Trial shall be at such Place or Places as the Congress may by Law have directed.*[16]

This Article, which also establishes the judicial branch, mandates (note the use of the word "shall" in the text) that all crimes will be tried by juries. This is not the case with most civil claims, which generally include a "right" to a jury at the request of the one of the parties.

The Seventh Amendment states:

> *In suits at common law, where the value in controversy shall exceed twenty dollars, the right of trial by jury shall be preserved, and no fact tried by a jury, shall be otherwise reexamined in any court of the United States, than according to the rules of the common law.*[17]

This Amendment refers to state civil trials and gives any defendant the right to have his or her case heard by a jury. The second clause of this Amendment prohibits appellate courts from re-examining facts that have already been established at the jury trial.

Very few challenges to the jury requirement have been brought to the Supreme Court. One of note involved a woman suing her landlord under the 1968 Civil Rights Act. The woman sued in tort under the Act, claiming that the landlord denied her rental application on the basis of her race. The defendant landlord requested a jury but the trial court denied his request, suggesting that the claim under the Act was for injunctive relief, which is traditionally an equitable claim and not a legal claim. The Seventh Amendment clearly refers to legal claims and not to equitable claims. But the Supreme Court disagreed with the trial court's reasoning.

Curtis v. Loether [18]

MR. JUSTICE MARSHALL delivered the opinion of the Court.

Section 812 of the Civil Rights Act of 1968, 82 Stat. 88, 42 U.S. C. § 3612, authorizes private plaintiffs to bring civil actions to redress violations of Title VIII, the fair housing provisions of the Act, and provides that "the court may grant as relief, as it deems appropriate, any permanent or temporary injunction, temporary restraining order, or other order, and may award to the plaintiff actual damages and not more than $ 1,000 punitive damages, together with court costs and reasonable attorney fees. . . . " The question presented in this case is whether the Civil Rights Act or the Seventh Amendment requires a jury trial upon demand by one of the parties in an action for damages and injunctive relief under this section.

Petitioner, a Negro woman, brought this action under § 812, claiming that respondents, who are white, had refused to rent an apartment to her because of her race, in violation of § 804 (a) of the Act, 42 U.S. C. § 3604 (a). In her complaint she sought only injunctive relief and punitive damages; a claim for compensatory damages was later added. After an evidentiary hearing, the District Court granted preliminary injunctive relief, enjoining the respondents from renting the apartment in question to anyone else pending the trial on the merits. This injunction was dissolved some five months later with the petitioner's consent, after she had finally obtained other housing, and the case went to trial on the issues of actual and punitive damages.

Respondents made a timely demand for jury trial in their answer. The District Court, however, held that jury trial was neither authorized by Title VIII nor required by the Seventh Amendment, and denied the jury request. Rogers *v.* Loether, *312 F.Supp. 1008 (ED Wis. 1970). After trial on the merits, the District Judge found that respondents had in fact discriminated against petitioner on account of her race. Although he found no actual damages, see n. 1,* supra, *he awarded $ 250 in punitive damages, denying petitioner's request for attorney's fees and court costs.*

The Court of Appeals reversed on the jury trial issue. Rogers *v.* Loether, *467 F.2d 1110 (CA7 1972). After an extended analysis, the court concluded essentially that the Seventh Amendment gave respondents the right to a jury trial in this action, and therefore interpreted the statute to authorize jury trials so as to eliminate any question of its constitutionality. In view of the importance of the jury trial issue in the administration and enforcement of Title VIII and the diversity of views in the lower courts on the question, we granted certiorari, 412 U.S. 937 (1973). We affirm.*

The legislative history on the jury trial question is sparse, and what little is available is ambiguous. There seems to be some indication that supporters of Title VIII were concerned that the possibility of racial prejudice on juries might reduce the effectiveness of civil rights damages actions. On the other hand, one bit of testimony during committee hearings indicates an awareness that jury trials would have to be afforded in damages actions under Title VIII. Both petitioner and respondents have presented plausible arguments from the wording and construction of § 812. We see no point to giving extended consideration to these arguments, however, for we think it is clear that the Seventh Amendment entitles either party to demand a jury trial in an action for damages in the federal courts under § 812.

The Seventh Amendment provides that "in suits at common law, where the value in controversy shall exceed twenty dollars, the right of trial by jury shall be preserved." Although the thrust of the Amendment was to preserve the right to jury trial as it existed in 1791, it has long been settled that the right extends beyond the common-law forms of action recognized at that time. Mr. Justice Story established the basic principle in 1830:

> *The phrase "common law," found in this clause, is used in contradistinction to equity, and admiralty, and maritime jurisprudence. . . . By* common law, *[the Framers of the Amendment] meant . . . not merely suits, which the* common *law recognized among its old and settled proceedings, but suits in which* legal *rights were to be ascertained and determined, in contradistinction to those where equitable rights alone were recognized, and equitable remedies were administered. . . . In a just sense, the amendment then may well be construed to embrace all suits which are not of equity and admiralty jurisdiction, whatever might be the peculiar form which they may assume to settle legal rights.*
>
> *Parsons* v. *Bedford,* 3 Pet. 433, 446–447 (1830) (emphasis in original)

Petitioner nevertheless argues that the Amendment is inapplicable to new causes of action created by congressional enactment. As the Court of Appeals observed, however, we have considered the applicability of the constitutional right to jury trial in actions enforcing statutory rights "as a matter too obvious to be doubted." 467 F.2d, at 1114. Although the Court has apparently never discussed the issue at any length, we have often found the Seventh Amendment applicable to causes of action based on statutes. See, e.g., Dairy Queen, Inc. *v.* Wood, *369 U.S. 469, 477 (1962) (trademark laws);* Hepner *v.* United States, *213 U.S. 103, 115 (1909) (immigration laws); cf.* Fleitmann *v.* Welsbach Street Lighting Co., *240 U.S. 27 (1916) (antitrust laws), and the discussion of* Fleitmann *in* Ross *v.* Bernhard, *396 U.S. 531, 535–536 (1970). Whatever doubt may have existed should now be dispelled. The Seventh Amendment does apply to actions enforcing statutory rights, and requires a jury trial upon demand, if the statute creates legal rights and remedies, enforceable in an action for damages in the ordinary courts of law.*

NLRB v. Jones & Laughlin Steel Corp., *301 U.S. 1 (1937), relied on by petitioner, lends no support to her statutory-rights argument. The Court there upheld the award of backpay without jury trial in an NLRB unfair labor practice proceeding, rejecting a Seventh Amendment claim on the ground that the case involved a "statutory proceeding" and "not a suit at common law or in the nature of such a suit."* Id., *at 48.* Jones & Laughlin *merely stands for the proposition that the Seventh Amendment is generally inapplicable in administrative proceedings, where jury trials would be incompatible with the whole concept of administrative adjudication and would substantially interfere with the NLRB's role in the statutory scheme.* Katchen v. Landy, *382 U.S. 323 (1966), also relied upon by petitioner, is to like effect. There the Court upheld, over a Seventh Amendment challenge, the Bankruptcy Act's grant of summary jurisdiction to the bankruptcy court over the trustee's action to compel a claimant to surrender a voidable preference; the Court recognized that a bankruptcy court has been traditionally viewed as a court of equity, and that jury trials would "dismember" the statutory scheme of the Bankruptcy Act.* Id., *at 339. See also* Guthrie National Bank v. Guthrie, *173 U.S. 528 (1899). These cases uphold congressional power to entrust enforcement of statutory rights to an administrative process or specialized court of equity free from the strictures of the Seventh Amendment. But when Congress provides for enforcement of statutory rights in an ordinary civil action in the district courts, where there is obviously no functional justification for denying the jury trial right, a jury trial must be available if the action involves rights and remedies of the sort typically enforced in an action at law.*

We think it is clear that a damages action under § 812 is an action to enforce "legal rights" within the meaning of our Seventh Amendment decisions. See, e.g., Ross v. Bernhard, supra, *at 533, 542;* Dairy Queen, Inc. v. Wood, supra, *at 476–477. A damages action under the statute sounds basically in tort—the statute merely defines a new legal duty and authorizes the courts to compensate a plaintiff for the injury caused by the defendant's wrongful breach. As the Court of Appeals noted, this cause of action is analogous to a number of tort actions recognized at common law. More important, the relief sought here—actual and punitive damages—is the traditional form of relief offered in the courts of law.*

We need not, and do not, go so far as to say that any award of monetary relief must necessarily be "legal" relief. See, e.g., Mitchell v. DeMario Jewelry, Inc., *361 U.S. 288 (1960);* Porter v. Warner Holding Co., *328 U.S. 395 (1946). A comparison of Title VIII with Title VII of the Civil Rights Act of 1964, where the courts of appeals have held that jury trial is not required in an action for reinstatement and backpay, is instructive, although we of course express no view on the jury trial issue in that context. In Title VII cases the courts of appeals have characterized backpay as an integral part of an equitable remedy, a form of restitution. But the statutory language on which this characterization is based—*

> *The court may enjoin the respondent from engaging in such unlawful employment practice, and order such affirmative action as may be appropriate, which may include, but is not limited to, reinstatement or hiring of employees, with or without back pay . . ., or any other equitable relief as the court deems appropriate, 42 U.S.C. § 2000e-5 (g) (1970 ed., Supp. II)—*

contrasts sharply with § 812's simple authorization of an action for actual and punitive damages. In Title VII cases, also, the courts have relied on the fact that the decision whether to award backpay is committed to the discretion of the trial judge. There is no comparable discretion here: if a plaintiff proves unlawful discrimination and actual damages, he is entitled to judgment for that amount. Nor is there any sense in which the award here can be viewed as requiring the defendant to disgorge funds wrongfully withheld from the plaintiff. Whatever may be the merit of the "equitable" characterization in Title VII cases, there is surely no basis for characterizing the award of compensatory and punitive damages here as equitable relief.

We are not oblivious to the force of petitioner's policy arguments. Jury trials may delay to some extent the disposition of Title VIII damages actions. But Title VIII actions seeking only equitable relief will be unaffected, and preliminary injunctive relief remains available without a jury trial even in damages actions. Dairy Queen, Inc. v. Wood, *369 U.S., at 479 n. 20. Moreover, the statutory requirement of expedition of § 812 actions, 42 U.S. C. § 3614, applies equally to jury and nonjury trials. We recognize, too, the possibility that jury prejudice may deprive a victim of discrimination of the verdict to which he or she is entitled. Of course, the trial judge's power to direct a verdict, to grant judgment notwithstanding the verdict, or to grant a new trial provides substantial protection against this risk, and respondents' suggestion that jury trials will expose a broader segment of the populace to the example of the federal civil rights laws in operation has some force. More fundamentally, however, these considerations are insufficient to overcome the clear command of the Seventh Amendment.*

The decision of the Court of Appeals must be Affirmed.

What we learn from the *Loether* case is that the American right to a jury trial extends to both law and equity claims in civil lawsuits. Whether the party is seeking injunctive relief or money damages, federal courts must provide the parties with access to a jury if they do desire.

Can you waive your right to a jury in a criminal trial if you choose to do so? Yes, so long as you do so knowingly and you receive the consent of the prosecutor and the judge. The courts have made clear that it is permissible for a court to deny a request to dismiss a jury, because the Constitution only guarantees a right to a jury, not a right to trial without a jury.[19] In the following case, the court considered whether a defendant could reduce the number of jurors from the constitutionally guaranteed twelve to eleven.

Patton v. United States[20]

MR. JUSTICE SUTHERLAND delivered the opinion of the Court.

The defendants (plaintiffs in error) were indicted in a federal district court, charged with conspiring to bribe a federal prohibition agent, a crime punishable by imprisonment in a federal penitentiary for a term of years. A jury of twelve men was duly impaneled. The trial began on October 19, 1927, and continued before the jury of twelve until October 26 following, at which time one of the jurors, because of severe illness, became unable to serve further as a juror. Thereupon it was stipulated in open court by the government and counsel for defendants, defendants personally assenting thereto, that the trial should proceed with the remaining eleven jurors. To this stipulation the court consented after stating that the defendants and the government both were entitled to a constitutional jury of twelve, and that the absence of one juror would result in a mistrial unless both sides should waive all objections and agree to a trial before the remaining eleven jurors. Following this statement, the stipulation was renewed in open court by all parties. During the colloquy counsel for defendants stated that he had personally conferred with all counsel and with each of the defendants individually, and it was the desire of all to finish the trial of the case with the eleven jurors if the defendants could waive the presence of the twelfth juror.

The trial was concluded on the following day, and a verdict of guilty was rendered by the eleven jurors. Each of the defendants was sentenced to terms of imprisonment in the penitentiary on the several counts of the indictment. An appeal was taken to the circuit court of appeals upon the ground that the defendants had no power to waive their constitutional right to a trial by a jury of twelve persons.

The court below, being in doubt as to the law applicable to the situation thus presented, and desiring the instruction of this court, has certified the following question:

> *After the commencement of a trial in a Federal Court before a jury of twelve men upon an indictment charging a crime, punishment for which may involve a penitentiary sentence, if one juror becomes incapacitated and unable to further proceed with his work as a juror, can defendant or defendants*

> *and the Government through its official representative in charge of the case consent to the trial proceeding to a finality with eleven jurors, and can defendant or defendants thus waive the right to a trial and verdict by a constitutional jury of twelve men?*

The question thus submitted is one of great importance, in respect of which there are differences of opinion among the various lower federal and state courts; but which this court thus far has not been required definitely to answer. There are, however, statements in some of our former opinions, which, if followed, would require a negative answer. These are referred to and relied upon by the defendants.

The federal Constitution contains two provisions relating to the subject. Article III, Section 2, Clause 3 provides:

> *The trial of all crimes, except in cases of impeachment, shall be by jury; and such trial shall be held in the State where the said crimes shall have been committed; but when not committed within any State, the trial shall be at such place or places as the Congress may by law have directed.*

The Sixth Amendment provides:

> *In all criminal prosecutions, the accused shall enjoy the right to a speedy and public trial, by an impartial jury of the State and district wherein the crime shall have been committed, which district shall have been previously ascertained by law, and to be informed of the nature and cause of the accusation; to be confronted with the witnesses against him; to have compulsory process for obtaining witnesses in his favor, and to have the assistance of counsel for his defense.*

Passing for later consideration the question whether these provisions, although varying in language, should receive the same interpretation, and whether taken together or separately the effect is to guaranty a right or establish a tribunal as an indispensable part of the government structure, we first inquire what is embraced by the phrase "trial by jury." That it means a trial by jury as understood and applied at common law, and includes all the essential elements as they were recognized in this country and England when the Constitution was adopted, is not open to question. Those elements were—(1) that the jury should consist of twelve men, neither more nor less; (2) that the trial should be in the presence and under the superintendence of a judge having power to instruct them as to the law and advise them in respect of the facts; and (3) that the verdict should be unanimous.

As to the first of these requisites, it is enough to cite Thompson v Utah, *170 U.S. 343, 350, where this court reversed the conviction of a defendant charged with grand larceny by a jury of eight men, saying:*

"It must consequently be taken that the word 'jury' and the words 'trial by jury' were placed in the Constitution of the United States with reference to the meaning affixed to them in the law as it was in this country and in England at the time of the adoption of that instrument; and that when Thompson committed the offence of grand larceny in the Territory of Utah—which was under the complete jurisdiction of the United States for all purposes of government and legislation—the supreme law of the land required that he should be tried by a jury composed of not less than twelve persons."

The second requisite was expressly dealt with in Capital Traction Company v. Hof, *174 U.S. 1, 13–16, where it is said:*

> *"Trial by jury," in the primary and usual sense of the term at the common law and in the American constitutions, is not merely a trial by a jury of twelve men before an officer vested with authority to cause them to be summoned and empanelled, to administer oaths to them and to the constable in charge, and to enter judgment and issue execution on their verdict; but it is a trial by a jury of twelve men, in the presence and under the superintendence of a judge empowered to instruct them on the law and to advise them on the*

> *facts, and (except on acquittal of a criminal charge) to set aside their verdict if in his opinion it is against the law or the evidence. This proposition has been so generally admitted, and so seldom contested, that there has been little occasion for its distinct assertion.*

The third requisite was held essential in American Publishing Company v. Fisher, *166 U.S. 464, 468;* Springville v. Thomas, *166 U.S. 707;* Maxwell v. Dow, *176 U.S. 581, 586.*

These common law elements are embedded in the constitutional provisions above quoted, and are beyond the authority of the legislative department to destroy or abridge. What was said by Mr. Justice Brewer in American Publishing Company v. Fisher, supra, *with respect to the requirement of unanimity, is applicable to the other elements as well:*

> *Whatever may be true as to legislation which changes any mere details of a jury trial, it is clear that a statute which destroys this substantial and essential feature thereof is one abridging the right.*

Any such attempt is vain and ineffectual, whatever form it may take. See In re Debs, *158 U.S. 564, 594.*

The foregoing principles, while not furnishing a precise basis for an answer to the question here presented, have the useful effect of disclosing the nature and scope of the problem, since they demonstrate the unassailable integrity of the establishment of trial by jury in all its parts, and make clear that a destruction of one of the essential elements has the effect of abridging the right in contravention of the Constitution. It follows that we must reject in limine *the distinction sought to be made between the effect of a complete waiver of a jury and consent to be tried by a less number than twelve, and must treat both forms of waiver as in substance amounting to the same thing. In other words, an affirmative answer to the question certified logically requires the conclusion that a person charged with a crime punishable by imprisonment for a term of years may, consistently with the constitutional provisions already quoted, waive trial by a jury of twelve and consent to a trial by any lesser number, or by the court without a jury.*

We are not unmindful of the decisions of some of the state courts holding that it is competent for the defendant to waive the continued presence of a single juror who has become unable to serve, while at the same time denying or doubting the validity of a waiver of a considerable number of jurors, or of a jury altogether. See, for example, State v. Kaufman, *51 Iowa 578, 580, with which compare* State v. Williams, *195 Iowa 374;* Commonwealth ex rel. Ross v. Egan, *281 Pa. 251, 256, with which compare* Commonwealth v. Hall, *291 Pa. 341. But in none of these cases are we able to find any persuasive ground for the distinction.*

Other state courts, with, we think, better reason, have adopted a contrary view. In State v. Baer, *103 Ohio St. 585, a person charged with manslaughter had been convicted by eleven jurors. The trial began with a jury of twelve, but, one of the jurors becoming incapable of service, the trial was concluded with the remaining eleven. In disposing of the case, the state supreme court thought it necessary to consider the broad question (p. 589): ". . . whether the right of trial by jury, as guaranteed by Sections 5 and 10 of the Bill of Rights, can be waived." After an extensive review of the authorities and a discussion of the question on principle, the court concluded that since it was permissible for an accused person to plead guilty and thus waive* any *trial, he must necessarily be able to waive a* jury *trial.*

In Jennings v. State, *134 Wis. 307, 309, where, again, a juror during the trial was excused from service because of illness, and the case was continued and concluded before the remaining eleven, the Supreme Court of Wisconsin also disposed of the case as involving the power of the defendant to waive a jury altogether, saying:*

> *It seems necessarily to follow that if a person on trial in a criminal case has no power to waive a jury he has no right to be tried by a less number than a common-law jury of twelve, and when he puts himself on the country it requires a jury of twelve to comply with the demands of the constitution. The fact that the jury in the instant case had the required number of twelve up to*

> *the stage in the trial when the cause was to be submitted to them under the instructions of the court cannot operate to satisfy the constitutional demand. At this point the trial was incomplete, for the very essential duty of having the jury deliberate upon the evidence and agree upon a verdict respecting defendant's guilt or innocence remained unperformed. Without the verdict of a jury of twelve it cannot be said to be a verdict of the jury required by the constitution. Such a verdict is illegal and insufficient to support a judgment.*

We deem it unnecessary to cite other cases which deal with the problem from the same point of view.

A constitutional jury means twelve men as though that number had been specifically named; and it follows that when reduced to eleven it ceases to be such a jury quite as effectively as though the number had been reduced to a single person. This conclusion seems self evident, and no attempt has been made to overthrow it save by what amounts to little more than a suggestion that by reducing the number of the jury to eleven or ten the infraction of the Constitution is slight, and the courts may be trusted to see that the process of reduction shall not be unduly extended. But the constitutional question cannot thus be settled by the simple process of ascertaining that the infraction assailed is unimportant when compared with similar but more serious infractions which might be conceived. To uphold the voluntary reduction of a jury from twelve to eleven upon the ground that the reduction—though it destroys the jury of the Constitution—is only a slight reduction, is not to interpret that instrument but to disregard it. It is not our province to measure the extent to which the Constitution has been contravened and ignore the violation, if in our opinion, it is not, relatively, as bad as it might have been.

We come, then, to the crucial inquiry: Is the effect of the constitutional provisions in respect of trial by jury to establish a tribunal as a part of the frame of government, or only to guaranty to the accused the right to such a trial? If the former, the question certified by the lower court must, without more, be answered in the negative.

Defendants strongly rely upon the language of this court in Thompson v. Utah, supra, *at page 353:*

> *It is said that the accused did not object, until after verdict, to a trial jury composed of eight persons, and therefore he should not be heard to say that his trial by such a jury was in violation of his constitutional rights. It is sufficient to say that it was not in the power of one accused of felony, by consent expressly given or by his silence, to authorize a jury of only eight persons to pass upon the question of his guilt. The law in force, when this crime was committed, did not permit any tribunal to deprive him of his liberty, except one constituted of a court and a jury of twelve persons.*

But this statement, though positive in form, is not authoritative. The case involved the validity of a statute dispensing with the common law jury of twelve and providing for trial by a jury of eight. There was no contention that the defendant, Thompson, had consented to the trial, but only that he had not objected until after verdict. The effect of an express consent on his part to a trial by a jury of eight was not involved—indeed he had been silent only under constraint of the statute—and what the court said in respect of that matter is, obviously, an obiter dictum.

Defendants also cite as supporting their contention two decisions of federal circuit courts of appeal, namely, Low v. United States, *169 Fed. 86; and* Dickinson v. United States, *159 Fed. 801.*

In the first of these cases the opinion, rendered by Judge Lurton, afterwards a justice of this court, definitely holds that the waiver of trial of a crime by jury involves setting aside the tribunal constituted by law for that purpose and the substitution by consent of one unknown to the law, and that this cannot be done by consent of the accused and the district attorney. "Undoubtedly," the opinion concludes, "the accused has a right to waive everything which pertains to form and much which is of the structure of a trial. But he may not waive that which concerns both himself and the public, nor any matter which involves fundamentally the jurisdiction of the court.

The jurisdiction of the court to pronounce a judgment or conviction for crime, when there has been a plea of not guilty, rests upon the foundation of a verdict by a jury. Without that basis the judgment is void." This is strong language from a judge whose opinion is entitled to great respect.

In the second case, involving the completion of a trial by consent with a jury of eleven persons, substantially the same was held; but in a scholarly and thoughtful dissenting opinion, Judge Aldrich reviews the common law practice upon the subject antedating the Constitution, and in the course of his opinion, after referring to Article III, Section 2, and the Sixth Amendment, says (pp. 813–814, 820–821):

> *The aim of the constitutional safeguards in question is a full, fair, and public trial, and one which shall reasonably and in all substantial ways safeguard the interests of the state and the life and liberty of accused parties. Whether the idea is expressed in words or not, as is done in some of the bills of rights and constitutions, a free and fair trial only means a trial as free and fair as the lot of humanity will admit.*
>
> *All will doubtless agree, at least the unquestioned authority is that way, that these protective provisions of the Constitution are not so imperative that an accused shall be tried by jury when he desires to plead guilty; or that his trial, in the event of trial, shall be held invalid for want of due process of law, based upon the ground that he was not confronted with his witnesses when he had waived that constitutional right and consented to the use of depositions; or because he had not had compulsory process for obtaining witnesses in his favor when he had waived that; or because he had not had the assistance of counsel when he had intelligently refused such constitutional privilege and insisted upon the right to go to trial without counsel; or upon the ground that he had not had a speedy trial when he had petitioned the court for delay; or that his trial was not public when he had consented to, or silently acquiesced in, a trial in a courthouse with a capacity for holding only 12 members of the public rather than 1200.*

Beyond question, the right of an accused in a case like this to have 12 jurors throughout is so far absolute as a constitutional right that he may have it by claiming it, or even by withholding consent to proceed without that number, and doubtless, under a constitutional government like ours, the interests of the community so far enter into any incidental departure from that number, in the course of the trial, as to require the discretionary approval of the court, and that the proper representative of the government should join the accused in consent.

. . . .

It is probable that the history and debates of the constitutional convention will not be found to sustain the idea that the constitutional safeguards in question were in any sense established as something necessary to protect the state or the community from the supposed danger that accused parties would waive away the interest which the government has in their liberties, and go to jail.

There is not now, and never was, any practical danger of that. Such a theory, at least in its application to modern American conditions, is based more upon useless fiction than upon reason. And when the idea of giving countenance to the right of waiver, as something necessary to a reasonable protection of the rights and liberties of accused, and as something intended to be practical and useful in the administration of the rights of the parties, has been characterized as involving innovation "highly dangerous," it would, as said by Judge Seevers in State v. Kaufman, *51 Iowa, 578, 581, 2 N.W. 275, 277, 33 Am. Rep. 148, "have been much more convincing and satisfactory if we had been informed why it would be highly dangerous."*

. . . .

Traced to its English origin, it would probably be found, so far as the right of waiver was there withheld from accused parties, that in a very large sense the reason for it was that conviction of crime, under the old English system, operated to outlaw and to attaint the blood and to work a forfeiture of official titles of inheritance, thus affecting the rights of third parties.

> *In every substantial sense our constitutional provisions in respect to jury trials in criminal cases are for the protection of the interests of the accused, and as such they may, in a limited and guarded measure, be waived by the party sought to be benefited.*

The record of English and colonial jurisprudence antedating the Constitution will be searched in vain for evidence that trial by jury in criminal cases was regarded as a part of the structure of government, as distinguished from a right or privilege of the accused. On the contrary, it uniformly was regarded as a valuable privilege bestowed upon the person accused of crime for the purpose of safeguarding him against the oppressive power of the King and the arbitrary or partial judgment of the court. Thus Blackstone, who held trial by jury both in civil and criminal cases in such esteem that he called it "the glory of the English law," nevertheless looked upon it as a "privilege," albeit "the most transcendent privilege which any subject can enjoy." Book III, p. 379. And Judge Story, writing at a time when the adoption of the Constitution was still in the memory of men then living, speaking of trial by jury in criminal cases said:

> *When our more immediate ancestors removed to America, they brought this great* privilege *with them, as their birthright and inheritance, as a part of that admirable common law which had fenced round and interposed barriers on every side against the approaches of arbitrary power. It is now incorporated into all our State constitutions as a fundamental* right, *and the Constitution of the United States would have been justly obnoxious to the most conclusive objection if it had not recognized and confirmed it in the most solemn terms.*
>
> 2 Story on the Constitution, § 1779

In the light of the foregoing it is reasonable to conclude that the framers of the Constitution simply were intent upon preserving the right of trial by jury primarily for the protection of the accused. If not, and their intention went beyond this and included the purpose of establishing the jury for the trial of crimes as an integral and inseparable part of the court, instead of one of its instrumentalities, it is strange that nothing to that effect appears in contemporaneous literature or in any of the debates or innumerable discussions of the time. This is all the more remarkable when we recall the minute scrutiny to which every provision of the proposed Constitution was subjected. The reasonable inference is that the concern of the framers of the Constitution was to make clear that the right of trial by jury should remain inviolable, to which end no language was deemed too imperative. That this was the purpose of the Third Article is rendered highly probable by a consideration of the form of expression used in the Sixth Amendment.

> *In all criminal prosecutions, the accused shall enjoy the right to a speedy and public trial, by an impartial jury . . .*

This provision, which deals with trial by jury clearly in terms of privilege, although occurring later than that in respect of jury trials contained in the original Constitution, is not to be regarded as modifying or altering the earlier provision; and there is no reason for thinking such was within its purpose. The first ten amendments and the original Constitution were substantially contemporaneous and should be construed in pari materia. *So construed, the latter provision fairly may be regarded as reflecting the meaning of the former. In other words, the two provisions mean substantially the same thing; and this is the effect of the holding of this court in* Callan v. Wilson, *127 U.S. 540, 549, where it is said:*

> *And we do not think that the amendment was intended to supplant that part of the third article which relates to trial by jury. There is no necessary conflict between them.*

Upon this view of the constitutional provisions we conclude that Article III, Section 2, is not jurisdictional, but was meant to confer a right upon the accused which he may forego at his election. To deny his power to do so, is to convert a privilege into an imperative requirement.

But the question remains whether the court is empowered to try the case without a jury; that is to say, whether Congress has vested jurisdiction to that end. We think it has, although some of the state, as well as some of the federal, decisions suggest a different conclusion.

By the Constitution, Article III, Section 1, the judicial power of the United States is vested in the Supreme Court and such inferior courts as Congress may from time to time ordain and establish. In pursuance of that authority, Congress, at an early day, established the district and circuit courts, and by § 24 of the Judicial Code (U.S. Code, Title 28, § 41 (2)), the circuit courts having been abolished, expressly conferred upon the district courts jurisdiction "of all crimes and offenses cognizable under the authority of the United States." This is a broad and comprehensive grant and gives the courts named power to try every criminal case cognizable under the authority of the United States, subject to the controlling provisions of the Constitution. In the absence of a valid consent the district court cannot proceed except with a jury, not because a jury is necessary to its jurisdiction, but because the accused is entitled by the terms of the Constitution to that mode of trial. Since, however, the right to a jury trial may be waived, it would be unreasonable to leave the court powerless to give effect to the waiver and itself dispose of the case. We are of opinion that the court has authority in the exercise of a sound discretion to accept the waiver, and, as a necessary corollary, to proceed to the trial and determination of the case with a reduced number or without a jury; and that jurisdiction to that end is vested by the foregoing statutory provisions. The power of waiver being established, this is the clear import of the decision of this court in Schick v. United States, *195 U.S. 65, 70–71.*

> *By section 563, Rev. Stat., [superseded by § 24, Judicial Code] the District Courts are given jurisdiction "of all crimes and offenses cognizable under the authority of the United States, committed within their respective districts, or upon the high seas, the punishment of which is not capital." There is no act of Congress requiring that the trial of all offenses shall be by jury,* and a court is fully organized and competent for the transaction of business without the presence of a jury.

See also In re Belt, *159 U.S. 95, and* Riddle v. Dyche, *262 U.S. 333, both of which are out of harmony with the notion that the presence of a jury is a constitutional prerequisite to the jurisdiction of the court in a criminal case. The first of these cases involved the validity of an act of Congress authorizing waiver of a jury in criminal cases in the District of Columbia. The Court of Appeals of that District upheld the statute in* Belt v. United States, *4 D.C. App. Cas. 25. Leave was asked of this court to file a petition for writ of* habeas corpus. *Upon this application, the question to be answered was (p. 97):*

"Does the ground of this application go to the jurisdiction or authority of the Supreme Court of the District, or rather is it not an allegation of mere error? If the latter, it cannot be reviewed in this proceeding. In re Schneider, *148 U.S. 162, and cases cited." After reviewing authorities, it was held that the Supreme Court of the District had jurisdiction to determine the validity of the act which authorized the waiver, and that its action could not be reviewed on* habeas corpus.

In the second case, Riddle, on habeas corpus, *assailed a conviction in a federal district court upon the ground that the jury was composed of only eleven men. This court held that the trial court had jurisdiction, and a record showing upon its face that a lawful jury had been impaneled, sworn, and charged could not be collaterally impeached. The remedy was by writ of error.*

This conclusion in respect of the jurisdiction of the courts, notwithstanding the peremptory words of the Third Article of the Constitution, is fortified by a consideration of certain provisions of the Judiciary Act of 1789. That act was passed shortly after the organization of the government under the Constitution, and on the day preceding the proposal of the first ten amendments by the first Congress. Among the members of that Congress were many who had participated in the convention which framed the Constitution and the act has always been considered, in relation to that instrument, as a contemporaneous exposition of the highest authority. Capital Traction Company v. Hof, supra, *pp. 9–10, and cases cited. Section 9 of that act provides that "the trial of issues in [of] fact, in the district courts, in all causes except civil causes of admiralty and maritime jurisdiction,* shall be by jury." *Section 12 provides that "the trial of issues in [of] fact in the circuit courts* shall, *in all suits, except those of equity, and of admiralty, and maritime jurisdiction,* be by jury."

It will be observed that this language is mandatory in form and is precisely the same as that of Article III, Section 2, of the Constitution. It is fair to assume that the framers of the statute, in using the words of the Constitution, intended they should have the same meaning; and if the purpose of the latter was jurisdictional, it is not easy to avoid the conclusion that the purpose of the former was the same. But this court has always held, beginning at an early day, that, notwithstanding the imperative language of the statute, it was competent for the parties to waive a trial by jury. The early cases are collected in a footnote to Kearney v. Case, *12 Wall. 275, 281, following the statement:*

> *Undoubtedly both the Judiciary Act and the amendment to the Constitution secured the* right *to either party in a suit at common law to a trial by jury, and we are also of opinion that the statute of 1789 intended to point out this as the mode of trial in issues of fact in such cases. Numerous decisions, however, had settled that this right to a jury trial might be waived by the parties, and that the judgment of the court in such cases should be valid.*

The Seventh Amendment, which is here referred to, provides, in respect of suits at common law involving a value exceeding twenty dollars, that "the right of trial by jury shall be preserved"; and it is significant that this language and the positive provision of the statute that "the trial of issues of fact . . . shall be by jury" were regarded as synonymous.

Another ground frequently relied upon for denying the power of a person accused of a serious crime to waive trial by jury is that such a proceeding is against public policy. The decisions are conflicting. The leading case in support of the proposition, and one which has influenced other decisions advancing similar views, is Cancemi v. The People, *18 N. Y. 128, 137–138. In that case Cancemi was indicted for the crime of murder. After a jury had been impaneled and sworn, and the trial begun, under a stipulation made by the prisoner and his counsel and counsel for the people, and with the express consent and request of the prisoner, a juror was withdrawn, and a verdict subsequently rendered by the remaining eleven jurors. On appeal a judgment based upon this verdict was reversed. The case was decided in 1858, and the question was regarded by the court as one of first impression. The following excerpt from the opinion indicates the basis of the decision:*

> *The state, the public, have an interest in the preservation of the liberties and the lives of the citizens, and will not allow them to be taken away "without due process of law" (Const., art. 1, § 6), when forfeited, as they may be, as a punishment for crimes. Criminal prosecutions proceed on the assumption of such a forfeiture, which, to sustain them, must be ascertained and declared as the law has prescribed. Blackstone (vol. 4, 189) says: "The king has an interest in the preservation of all his subjects." . . . Objections to jurors may be waived; the court may be substituted for triers to dispose of challenges to jurors; secondary in place of primary evidence may be received; admissions of facts are allowed; and in similar particulars, as well as in relation to mere formal proceedings generally, consent will render valid, what without it would be erroneous. A plea of guilty to any indictment, whatever may be the grade of the crime, will be received and acted upon if it is made clearly to appear that the nature and effect of it are understood by the accused. In such a case the preliminary investigation of a grand jury, with the admission of the accusation in the indictment, is supposed to be a sufficient safeguard to the public interests. But when issue is joined upon an indictment, the trial must be by the tribunal and in the mode which the constitution and laws provide, without any essential change. The public officer prosecuting for the people has no authority to consent to such a change, nor has the defendant.*
>
> *Applying the above reasoning to the present case, the conclusion necessarily follows, that the consent of the plaintiff in error*

> *to the withdrawal of one juror, and that the remaining eleven might render a verdict, could not lawfully be recognized by the court, at the circuit, and was a nullity. If a deficiency of one juror might be waived, there appears to be no good reason why a deficiency of eleven might not be; and it is difficult to say why, upon the same principle, the entire panel might not be dispensed with, and the trial committed to the court alone. It would be a highly dangerous innovation, in reference to criminal cases, upon the ancient and invaluable institution of trial by jury, and the constitution and laws establishing and securing that mode of trial, for the court to allow of any number short of a full panel of twelve jurors, and we think it ought not to be tolerated.*

A decision flatly to the contrary, and one fairly representative of others to the same effect, is State v. Kaufman, *51 Iowa 578. The defendant there was indicted for forgery. Upon the trial, one of the jurors, being ill, was discharged with the consent of the defendant, and the trial concluded with the remaining eleven. There was a verdict of guilty. Upon appeal the verdict was upheld. The authorities upon the question are reviewed, and in the course of the opinion the court says (pp. 579–580):*

> *A plea of guilty ordinarily dispenses with a jury trial, and it is thereby waived. This, it seems to us, effectually destroys the force of the thought that "the State, the public, have an interest in the preservation of the lives and the liberties of the citizens, and will not allow them to be taken away without due process of law." The same thought is otherwise expressed by Blackstone, vol. 4, p. 189, that "the king has an interest in the preservation of all his subjects."*
>
> *It matters not whether the defendant is, in fact, guilty; the plea of guilty is just as effectual as if such was the case. Reasons other than the fact that he is guilty may induce a defendant to so plead, and thereby the State may be deprived of the services of the citizen, and yet the State never actually interferes in such case, and the right of the defendant to so plead has never been doubted. He must be permitted to judge for himself in this respect. So in the case at bar. The defendant may have consented to be*

> *tried by eleven jurors, because his witnesses were then present, and he might not be able to get them again, or that it was best he should be tried by the jury as thus constituted. Why should he not be permitted to do so? Why hamper him in this respect? Why restrain his liberty or right to do as he believed to be for his interest? Whatever rule is adopted affects not only the defendant, but all others similarly situated, no matter how much they may desire to avail themselves of the right to do what the defendant desires to repudiate. We are unwilling to establish such a rule.*

Referring to the statement in the Cancemi *case, that it would be a highly dangerous innovation to allow any number short of a full panel of twelve jurors and one not to be tolerated, it is said (p. 581):*

> *This would have been much more convincing and satisfactory if we had been informed why it would be 'highly dangerous,' and should 'not be tolerated,' or, at least, something which had a tendency in that direction. For if it be true, as stated, it certainly would not be difficult to give a satisfactory reason in support of the strong language used.*

See also State v. Sackett, *39 Minn. 69, where the court concludes its discussion of the subject by saying (p. 72):*

> *The wise and beneficent provisions found in the constitution and statutes, designed for the welfare and protection of the accused, may be waived, in matters of form and substance, when jurisdiction has been acquired, and within such limits as the trial court, exercising a sound discretion in behalf of those before it, may permit. The defendants, having formally waived a juror, and stipulated to try their case with 11, cannot now claim that there was a fatal irregularity in their trial.*

It is difficult to see why the fact, frequently suggested, that the accused may plead guilty and thus dispense with a trial altogether, does not effectively disclose the fallacy of the public policy contention; for if the state may interpose the claim of public interest between the accused and his desire to waive a jury trial, a fortiori *it should be able to interpose a like claim between him and his determination to avoid any form of trial by admitting his guilt. If he be free to decide the question for himself in the latter case, notwithstanding the interest of society in the preservation of his life and liberty, why should he be denied the power to do so in the former? It is no answer to say that by pleading guilty there is nothing left for a jury to try, for that simply ignores the question, which is not what is the effect of the plea? the answer to which is fairly obvious, but, in view of the interest of the public in the life and liberty of the accused, can the plea be accepted and acted upon, or must the question of guilt be submitted to a jury at all events? Moreover, the suggestion is wholly beside the point, which is, that public policy is not so inconsistent as to permit the accused to dispense with* every *form of trial by a plea of guilty, and yet forbid him to dispense with a* particular *form of trial by consent.*

The truth is that the theory of public policy embodies a doctrine of vague and variable quality, and, unless deducible in the given circumstances from constitutional or statutory provisions, should be accepted as the basis of a judicial determination, if at all, only with the utmost circumspection. The public policy of one generation may not, under changed conditions, be the public policy of another.

It may be conceded, at least generally, that under the rule of the common law the accused was not permitted to waive trial by jury, as generally he was not permitted to waive any right which was intended for his protection. Nevertheless, in the Colonies such a waiver and trial by the court without a jury was by no means unknown, as the many references contained in the brief of the Solicitor General conclusively show. But this phase of the matter we do not stop to consider, for the rule of the common law, whether exclusive or subject to exceptions, was justified by conditions which no longer exist; and as the Supreme Court of Nevada well said in Reno Smelting Works v. Stevenson, *20 Nev. 269, 279:*

> *It is contrary to the spirit of the common law itself to apply a rule founded on a particular reason to a law when that reason utterly fails—*cessante ratione legis, cessat ipsa lex.

*The maxim seems strikingly apposite to the question here under review. Among other restraints at common law, the accused could not testify in his own behalf; in felonies he was not allowed counsel (IV Sharswood's Blackstone, 355, Note 14), the judge in such cases occupying the place of counsel for the prisoner, charged with the responsibility of seeing that the prisoner did not suffer from lack of other counsel (*id.*); and conviction of crime worked an attaint and forfeiture of official titles of inheritance, which, as Judge Aldrich points out (quotation* supra*), constituted in a large sense the reason for withholding from accused parties the right of waiver.*

These conditions have ceased to exist, and with their disappearance justification for the old rule no longer rests upon a substantial basis. In this respect we fully agree with what was said by the Supreme Court of Wisconsin in Hack v. State*, 141 Wis. 346, 351–352:*

> *The ancient doctrine that the accused could waive nothing was unquestionably founded upon the anxiety of the courts to see that no innocent man should be convicted. It arose in those days when the accused could not testify in his own behalf, was not furnished counsel, and was punished, if convicted, by the death penalty or some other grievous punishment out of all proportion to the gravity of his crime. Under such circumstances it was well, perhaps, that such a rule should exist, and well that every technical requirement should be insisted on, when the state demanded its meed of blood. Such a course raised up a sort of a barrier which the court could utilize when a prosecution was successful which ought not to have been successful, or when a man without money, without counsel, without ability to summon witnesses, and not permitted to tell his own story, had been unjustly convicted, but yet under the ordinary principles of waiver, as applied to civil matters, had waived every defect in the proceedings.*
>
> *Thanks to the humane policy of the modern criminal law we have changed all these conditions. The man now charged with crime is furnished the most complete opportunity for making*

> *his defense. He may testify in his own behalf; if he be poor, he may have counsel furnished him by the state and may have his witnesses summoned and paid for by the state; not infrequently he is thus furnished counsel more able than the attorney for the state. In short, the modern law has taken as great pains to surround the accused person with the means to effectively make his defense as the ancient law took pains to prevent that consummation. The reasons which in some sense justified the former attitude of the courts have therefore disappeared, save perhaps in capital cases, and the question is, Shall we adhere to the principle based upon conditions no longer existing? No sound reason occurs to us why a person accused of a lesser crime or misdemeanor, who comes into court with his attorney, fully advised of all his rights and furnished with every means of making his defense, should not be held to waive a right or privilege for which he does not ask, just as a party to a civil action waives such a right by not asking for it.*

The view that power to waive a trial by jury in criminal cases should be denied on grounds of public policy must be rejected as unsound.

It is not denied that a jury trial may be waived in the case of petty offenses, but the contention is that the rule is otherwise in the case of crimes of the magnitude of the one here under consideration. There are decisions to that effect and also decisions to the contrary. The conflict is marked and direct. Schick v. United States, supra, *is thought to favor the contention. There the prosecution was for a violation of the Oleomargarine Act (24 Stat. 209), punishable by fine only. By agreement in writing a jury was waived and the issue submitted to the court. Judgment was for the United States. This court held that the offense was a petty one and sustained the waiver. It was said that the word "crimes" in Article III, Section 2, of the Constitution, should be read in the light of the common law, and so read, it does not include petty offenses; and that neither the constitutional provisions nor any rule of public policy prevented the defendant from waiving a jury trial. The question whether the power of waiver extended to serious offenses was not directly involved and is not concluded by that decision. Mr. Justice Harlan, in a dissenting opinion, after reviewing the authorities, concluded (p. 83) that "The grounds upon which the decisions rest are, upon principle, applicable alike in cases of felonies and misdemeanors, although the consequences to the accused may be more evident as well as more serious in the former than in the latter cases."*

Although we reject the general view of the dissenting opinion that a waiver of jury trial is not valid in any criminal case, we accept the foregoing statement as entirely sound. We are unable to find in the decisions any convincing ground for holding that a waiver is effective in misdemeanor cases but not effective in the case of felonies. In most of the decisions no real attempt is made to establish a distinction, beyond the assertion that public policy favors the power of waiver in the former but denies it in the latter because of the more serious consequences in the form of punishment which may ensue. But that suggested differentiation, in the light of what has now been said, seems to us more fanciful than real. The Schick *case, it is true, dealt with a petty offense, but, in view of the conclusions we have already reached and stated, the observations of the court (pp. 71–72) have become equally pertinent where a felony is involved:*

> *Article six of the amendments, as we have seen, gives the accused a right to a trial by jury. But the same article gives him the further right "to be confronted with the witnesses against him . . . and to have the assistance of counsel." Is it possible that an accused cannot admit and be bound by the admission that a witness not present would testify to certain facts? Can it be that if he does not wish the assistance of counsel and waives it, the trial is invalid? It seems only necessary to ask these questions to answer them. When there is no constitutional or statutory mandate, and no public policy prohibiting, an accused may waive any privilege which he is given the right to enjoy.*

In Commonwealth v. Beard, *48 Pa. Super. Ct. 319, the prosecution was for conspiracy, and there, as here, one of the jurors was discharged and the trial concluded with the remaining eleven.*

Judgment on a verdict of conviction was sustained. The court, after reviewing the conflicting decisions, was unable to find any good reason for differentiating in the matter of waiver between the two classes of crimes. We fully endorse its concluding words upon that subject (pp. 323–324):

> *It surely cannot be true that the public is interested in the protection of an accused in proportion to the magnitude of his offending—that its solicitude goes out to the great offender but not to the small—that there is a difference in point of sacredness between constitutional rights when asserted by one charged with a grave crime and when asserted by one charged with a lesser one. Hence, when it is held in* Schick v. U.S., *195 U.S. 65 (24 Sup. Ct. Reptr. 826), that in trials for the lowest grades of offenses the accused may waive, not only the continued presence of the full number of jurors required to make up a jury, but the right to trial by jury, the only possible conclusion is that the purely theoretical element of public concern, as potential to override the accused's own free choice and render him effectually unfree even before conviction and sentence, cannot be regarded as in reality much of a factor in any case.*

This view of the matter subsequently had the approval of the supreme court of the state in Commonwealth ex rel. Ross v. Egan, *281 Pa. 251. After noting the conflict of authority, and that a waiver has been held to be effective in a number of states which are named, it is there said (pp. 255, 256, 257):*

> *A defendant is supposed to understand his rights, and may be aided, if he so desires, by counsel to advise him. There are many legal provisions for his security and benefit which he may dispense with absolutely, as, for instance, his right to plead guilty and submit to sentence without any trial whatsoever.*
>
> . . . .
>
> *The theory upon which the opposing cases are decided seems to rest on the proposition that society at large is as much interested in an impartial trial of a defendant, who may be sentenced to*

> *imprisonment, as he himself is, and therefore no permission to waive any right, when charged with a felony, should be accorded to him. There may be reason for applying this rule to capital cases, as has been done in Pennsylvania, but such a principle ought not to be invoked to relieve those charged with lesser offenses, such as larceny (though technically denominated a felony), from the consequences of their own voluntary act, and where it appears by the record that consent to the course pursued was freely given, the defendant should not be heard thereafter to complain.*
>
> *The solution of the question depends upon the determination whether a trial by less than twelve is an irregularity or a nullity. If the latter be held, no sentence imposed may be sustained, but the contrary is true if the former and correct conclusion be reached. In the case of misdemeanors, the Superior Court has sustained the sentences where a voluntary waiver appeared:* Com. v. Beard, supra. *No real justification for a different decision in the case of felonies, not capital, can be supported.*

See also Commonwealth v. Rowe, *257 Mass. 172, 174–176;* State v. Ross, *47 S.D. 188, 192–193, involving a misdemeanor, but followed in* State v. Tiedeman, *49 S.D. 356, 360, involving a felony. In affirming the power of the defendant in any criminal case to waive a trial by a constitutional jury and submit to trial by a jury of less than twelve persons, or by the court, we do not mean to hold that the waiver must be put into effect at all events. That perhaps sufficiently appears already. Trial by jury is the normal and, with occasional exceptions, the preferable mode of disposing of issues of fact in criminal cases above the grade of petty offenses. In such cases the value and appropriateness of jury trial have been established by long experience, and are not now to be denied. Not only must the right of the accused to a trial by a constitutional jury be jealously preserved, but the maintenance of the jury as a fact finding body in criminal cases is of such importance and has such a place in our traditions, that, before any waiver can become effective, the consent of government counsel and the sanction of the court must be had, in addition to the express and intelligent consent of the defendant. And the duty of the trial court in that regard is not to be discharged as a mere matter of rote, but with sound and advised discretion, with an eye to avoid unreasonable or undue departures from that mode of trial or from any of the essential elements thereof, and with a caution increasing in degree as the offenses dealt with increase in gravity.*

The question submitted must be answered in the affirmative.

It Is So Ordered

Trial juries are not the only types of juries established by the U.S. Constitution. At the time, there was concern that prosecutors in criminal trials might abuse their power by bringing charges against those who they sought to influence in some way. In a criminal case, the prosecutor maintains a great deal of discretion to decide when and if to file charges, even if substantial evidence exists against the potential defendant. Grand juries will be discussed in the next section.

Grand Juries

The grand jury was established in the common law around the same time as the trial jury by King Henry II (12th century). However, nearly every country today has eliminated the use of grand juries—that is, every country except the United States. The grand jury clause of the U.S. Constitution reads as follows:

No person shall be held to answer for a capital, or otherwise infamous crime, unless on a presentment or indictment of a grand jury, except in cases arising in the land or naval forces, or in the militia, when in actual service in time of war or public danger; nor shall any person be subject for the same offense to be twice put in jeopardy of life or limb; nor shall be compelled in any criminal case to be a witness against himself, nor be deprived of life, liberty, or property, without due process of law; nor shall private property be taken for public use, without just compensation.[21]

The original concept of the grand jury was to create a body that would investigate the evidence that would be proffered in a criminal case against a suspect (not yet a defendant). The grand jury, which was composed of between 12 and 23 citizens, heard arguments from the prosecutor and instructions from a judge regarding the threshold of evidence needed to "indict," or bring formal charges against the suspect, thereby turning the suspect into a defendant. The suspect had no opportunity to be heard at the grand jury hearing because he or she was not yet being charged with a crime and thus no defense was necessary. However, if the grand jury chose to indict, a petit jury would be empaneled and a jury trial would begin.

Historically, anyone could bring allegations to a grand jury against a criminal suspect. The grand jury would investigate, and then, if they chose to indict, the person bringing the allegations would be given legal authority to represent the state in the jury trial against the now defendant. This practice ceased with the establishment of state prosecutors, who are now the only officials empowered to establish a grand jury.

Today, the use of the grand jury is much more limited, often being established only for allegations of serious crimes and potentially damaging cases against politicians and other officials. It is a mechanism for the state to protect itself against unsubstantiated charges or prosecutions for purely political gains. However, the grand jury process has recently been criticized as a way for a prosecutor to protect public officials.

On August 9, 2014, in Ferguson, Missouri, black teenager Michael Brown was shot and killed by white police officer Darren Wilson. No video recording exists of the incident (unlike other incidents around the same time), so determining whether a crime was committed is limited exclusively to the evidence. If any charges would be brought against the officer for the shooting of Mr. Brown, those charges would be brought in state court. Accordingly, before bringing any charges, the state prosecutor chose to empanel a grand jury to review the evidence and determine if it was sufficient to proffer an indictment.

It is debatable whether a grand jury is necessary in cases like this. There is little doubt that a charge *could* be brought against

Officer Wilson in state court, where a petit jury would hear both sides of the case. And if the prosecutor chose to begin with a grand jury process and desired an indictment against the officer, it likely would have been an easy argument to make, especially given the lack of substantial evidence for or against the officer in this case. According to law professor Andrew Leipold, "If the prosecutor wants an indictment and doesn't get one, something has gone horribly wrong."[22] Former New York state chief judge Sol Wachtler even said that a prosecutor could persuade a grand jury to "indict a ham sandwich."[23] But in this case, the grand jury chose not to indict Officer Wilson, setting off a series of protests across the country.

What we learn about American legal reasoning from the Darren Wilson case is that the reliance by U.S. courts on the jury system can create often unpredictable results. The lack of indictment in Officer Wilson's case, an unappealable decision, reflects the power given to average citizens to determine whether or not to charge someone with a crime. Similar power is given to petit juries to determine the veracity of the parties' statements at both civil and criminal trials.

Bear in mind that juries may be avoidable. Courts of Chancery in Delaware, for instance, are trial courts that hear real estate, trusts, civil rights, and commercial litigation cases without juries. And in most state cases, a party can request a bench trial, thereby eliminating the need to empanel a jury (remember that the other party and the judge must agree).

The jury system is not unique to American courts. However, in most countries, it exists only for serious crimes.[24] Thus, the American judiciary's use of petit juries in civil cases as well as grand juries in some criminal cases sets it apart in international litigation and poses risks for parties unaware of the risks they face when leaving part of their fate in the hands of ordinary American citizens.

Notes

1 *Dienes Corp. v. Long Island R.R.*, 2002 U.S. Dist. LEXIS 6824, 47 U.C.C. Rep. Serv. 2d (Callaghan) 941 (E.D.N.Y. 2002).

2 Pub.L. 104–199, 110 Stat. 2419, enacted September 21, 1996, 1 U.S.C. § 7 and 28 U.S.C. § 1738C.

3 U.S. Const. Amend. X.
4 Note, though, Congress could attempt to pass new legislation in response to the decision.
5 *DeBoer v. Snyder*, Case No. 14–1321 (6th Cir. 2014) at 18.
6 Id.
7 Id. at 21.
8 Id. at 35.
9 Id. at 42.
10 Id. at 43.
11 Kedar Bhatia, *October Term 2012 summary memo*, SCOTUSblog, June 29, 2013 (10:25 AM), http://www.scotusblog.com/2013/06/october-term-2012-summary-memo/.
12 *Latta v. Otter*, No. 14–35420 (9th Cir. 2014) at 32–33.
13 Id. at 33.
14 Id. at 34.
15 W. Blackstone, *Commentaries on the Laws of England* *349–*350 (T. Cooley 4th ed. 1896).
16 U.S. Const. Art. III, § 2.
17 U.S. Const. Amend. VII.
18 *Curtis v. Loether*, 415 U.S. 189, 189–198, 94 S. Ct. 1005, 39 L. Ed. 2d 260, 1974 U.S. LEXIS 98, 2–18, 18 Fed. R. Serv. 2d (Callaghan) 189 (U.S. 1974).
19 *Singer v. United States*, 380 U.S. 24 (1965).
20 *Patton v. United States*, 281 U.S. 276 (1930).
21 U.S. Const. Amend. V.
22 Anthony L. Fisher, *Grand Juries Almost Never Fail to Indict, But they Did in Ferguson*, Hit & Run (blog), November 25, 2014, http://reason.com/blog/2014/11/25/grand-juries-almost-never-fail-to-indict.
23 January 1985 interview with the New York Daily News' Marcia Kramer and Frank Lombardi, ABA Journal, November 26, 2014, http://www.abajournal.com/news/article/grand_juries_almost_always_indict_federal_stats_show_is_there_a_cop_shootin/.
24 This includes Australia, Austria, Belgium, Canada, England, France, Greece, Hong Kong (carried over from English rule), India, Ireland, Italy, Japan, New Zealand, Norway (civil and criminal), Russia, Sweden (for fundamental rights only), and Switzerland.

2

THE COMMERCIAL HISTORY OF THE COMMON LAW

Students of civil law programs are taught very differently from those in common law programs, such as those in the United States. In a civil law program, emphasis is placed on memorization of statutes and ordinances in order to develop the ability to recall the applicable law to any given situation. In a common law program, emphasis is placed on the analytical process itself, using statutes and cases more as examples of effective (or ineffective) legal analysis rather than as outcomes to be memorized. There is no expectation in a common law system that the law will remain unchanged or that it is not open to new interpretations; in fact, quite the opposite is true. Common law lawyers are taught that they should use their legal analysis skills to apply the law in the most beneficial way for their case.

As discussed earlier in this book, there are benefits and drawbacks to each approach. But what is clear is that resulting principles have in many cases developed independently of one another, making the job of the cross-border lawyer particularly challenging. Take for a moment the concept of contract formation. One of the most fundamental tasks performed by international attorneys is ensuring that a cross-border contract is drafted in a way to both protect their client's interests and such that it will be enforced in the desired jurisdiction. As I will demonstrate in the following pages, the civil law approach that has historically relied on formalities to ensure proper formation of a contract is distinguishable from the common law approach that examines intent and action in lieu of formalities. Not only does this reflect a concern for international transactional attorneys, it also reflects the type of analysis that a common law lawyer will use in assessing the transaction itself.

Causa and Consideration

Common law contracts developed from merchant rules in the 11th century, when the Count of Flanders decentralized the court system to allow local tribunals to handle matters, including commercial contracts. From this point and through the abandonment of local courts in the late 15th century, only two actions were permitted under common law contract disputes—debt and covenant.[1] Debt contracts were explicit or implicit agreements to pay a fixed sum to another party. Covenant actions were for breaches of existing promises made under seal. Executory contracts—contracts that have been agreed upon but not yet fully performed—were not enforceable at this time. Thus, it was impossible at law in this era to force someone to comply with their contractual obligations, even if one party has already performed (but the other has not).

In medieval courts, the only way to enforce an executed contract was to prove that a promise was explicitly made to pay a debt to the promisee and to bring a writ of debt to the court. The defendant promisor could then request a "wager of law," which allowed him to testify to the court that he did not owe any such debt to the plaintiff. If the defendant produced 11 individuals to swear that they believed him, the case was dismissed.[2] It should be noted that this defense was never permitted in United States courts.[3]

Parties had great difficulty enforcing contracts in medieval courts due to their failure to recognize the existence of binding contracts based upon promises to perform. However, toward the middle of the 15th century, lawyers began utilizing a new cause of action—*assumpsit.* This was a claim made to enforce a contract, written or verbal, not under seal or recorded (as a debt contract might be). It served as an independent cause of action and could be brought, unlike a writ of debt, in front of a jury where wagers of law were not permitted.

The writ of *assumpsit* was not immediately recognized by the medieval courts in England. However, this changed with *Slade's Case* in 1602. In that case, John Slade brought an action in *assumpsit* against Humphrey Morley, claiming that Slade promised to sell and Morley promised to buy a crop of wheat and rye for £16. Morley reneged on the agreement and Slade sued. The case dragged on for six years until Chief Judge Lord Popham issued a written opinion formally recognizing the *assumpsit* cause of action:

> *every contract executory importeth in it self an Assumpsit, for when one agreeth to pay money, or to deliver anything, thereby he promiseth to pay, or deliver it; and therefore when one selleth any goods to another, and agreeth to deliver them at a day to come, and the other* ***in consideration thereof*** *promiseth to pay so much money to the other.*[4]

The legal claim of *assumpsit* quickly overtook the writ of debt as the primary action brought for breach of contract. This is the standard contract enforcement action that the common law courts still follow today (though it is no longer called *assumpsit*). It was this writ of *assumpsit* that led to the need for the concept of consideration.

Assumpsit was largely an action to enforce commercial contracts, which were often informal and executory. The common law courts were heavily influenced by merchants, which had been seeking recourse for breaches of executory contracts (where parties have not yet completed their performance) since the 11th century, and *assumpsit* provided such recourse. Facilitation of economic arrangements became the motivating factor in enforcing medieval contracts.

Though the 16th century English courts were willing to enforce these informal and executory contracts, they (and the merchants invoking these actions) were aware of the risk of making every agreement between parties a binding contract. And given the fact that the merchants engaged in these transactions had little opportunity to formalize the agreements in front of a notary, as was required under most civil law systems then under development, the courts chose instead to create a requirement that the parties bargained for their transaction in lieu of the formalities otherwise required.[5] Hence, the creation of consideration.

By the middle of the 19th century, courts recognized two forms of *assumpsit*—express and implied—as defined below in 1856:

> *An express assumpsit is where one undertakes verbally or in writing, not under seal, or by matter of record, to perform an act, or to pay a sum of money to another.*
>
> *An implied assumpsit is where one has not made any formal promise to do an act or to pay a sum of money to another, but who is presumed from his conduct to have assumed to do what is in point of law just and right . . . it is a rule that he who desires the antecedent, must abide by the consequent; as, if I receive a loaf of bread or a newspaper daily sent to my house without orders, and I use it without objection, I am presumed to have accepted the terms upon which the person sending it had in contemplation, that I should pay a fair price for it.*[6]

Though civil law jurisdictions never adopted consideration, similarities can be drawn between their doctrine of *causa* and the newly emerging common law doctrine of consideration.[7] Before explaining the similarities and differences between the two substantive legal concepts, it is important to understand the foundational differences between them. Consideration is a common law doctrine crafted by courts and by its nature, unlike the civil law, "that springs from statutes, regulations, and constitutional provisions."[8] In the civil law, what is "law" and what is a "contract" is determined by an exclusive list of legislative materials (e.g., statutes, regulations), and the function of courts and judges is merely to apply that "law" in a prescribed and technical manner.[9] As stated by authors John Henry Merryman and Rogelio Perez-Perdomo in their book *The Civil Law Tradition*, "[t]o the average judge, lawyer, or law student in [civil law countries], the traditional theory of sources of law represent the basic truth." Hence, *causa* as a requirement partly applies because it is statutorily required as a complete codification of the "law."[10]

The loose definition of *causa* in civil law jurisdictions would be party consent and lawful purpose. As an example of the civil law's statutory requirements, France's civil code requires "une cause licite dans l'obligation."[11] The provision translates to "a lawful purpose obliged" or the civil law requirement of *causa*.[12] While the requirement of consideration is often found in common law legislative materials, its definition and application to particular cases is often bound to prior case law. The differences in both the source of law and interpretation of the law are important to keep in mind when analyzing the doctrine of consideration and *causa*.

The doctrine of consideration and the legal requirement for *causa* both deal with the formation of lawful contracts. Civil law countries, at least theoretically, view their codifications of law as complete.[13] It follows that the determination as to whether a contract has formed will depend on the statutory requirements. As an example of the requirements to form a valid civil law contract, Article 1108 of the French *Code Civil* requires the following:

> *Quatre conditions sont essentialles pour la validite d'une convention:*
> (Four conditions are essential for the validity of an agreement)
> *Le consentement de la partie qui s'oblige;*
> (The consent of the obligated party)
> *Sa capacite de contracter;*
> (Its[, the obligated party's,] ability to contract)
> *Un object certain qui forma la matiere de l'engagement;*
> (Some object which formed the matter of commitment)
> *Une cause licite dans l'obligation.*
> (A lawful purpose obliged)[14]

Contrast these contractual validity requirements with the requirements in a common law jurisdiction, which include intent, offer, acceptance, and consideration. Consideration is described as the bargained-for-exchange between the parties and is often explained in terms of mutuality. It pits one against the other and requires a bargaining or negotiation process. *Causa* is a principle as much as it is a legal requirement for a contract. Its origins stem from the legal theory that a contract required both consent and some cause "that the law would respect."[15] Historically, the theory behind *causa* can be divided into two legal causes, one for gratuitous contracts and one for onerous contracts.[16] In the gratuitous contract there must be the *causa* of exercising liberality and conferring some benefit on another, and in the onerous contract there must be the *causa* of receiving the equivalent of what one gave up.[17] The Louisiana Civil Code defines *causa* as "the reason whereby a party obligates himself," hence it is often described as the contractual motive or purpose.[18]

Common law consideration and civil law *causa* do have important differences with respect to the answers these doctrines were created to solve. The common law focus on unenforceable promises is not as important in civil law.[19] Instead, consent takes an important role in determining whether a contract exists, as illustrated by its position as a requirement in the French *Code Civil* cited above (listed as the first requirement).[20] The common law focus on enforceable versus unenforceable requires that something be lacking as an element to deny certain contracts. Meanwhile, the civil law focus on the will merely requires compliance with the formalities dictated by code.

Similarly, determining what is enforceable versus unenforceable in a common law jurisdiction requires a level of latitude in judicial interpretation not found in civil law systems. Where "consent" is the metaphorical sun that contracts orbit around, judicial latitude takes on little importance. Consent or will in the civil law context may be negative—that is, it is assumed in the absence of fraud, mistake, or duress—or it may be positive, whereby the parties must show some objective manifestation of their will.[21]

The doctrine of consideration, though mentioned as early as 1602 in *Slade's Case*, was used interchangeably with the civil law doctrine of *causa* in prior English court decisions. In fact, Lord Mansfield attempted to eliminate the use of consideration as a requirement for a valid contract in an opinion issued in 1765: "I take it, that the ancient notion about the want of consideration was for the sake of evidence only; for when it is reduced into writing, as in covenants, specialties, bonds, etc., there was no objection to the want of consideration."[22] He went on to conclude, "[i]n commercial cases amongst merchants, the want of consideration is not an objection."[23]

However, Lord Mansfield's dismissal of consideration was short-lived. The need for consideration in contracts was reaffirmed ten years later in the case of *Rann v. Hughes*.[24] In that case, the court held "that every man is by the law of nature bound to fulfill his engagements. It is equally true that the law of [England] supplies no means, nor affords any remedy, to compel the performance of an agreement made without sufficient consideration."[25]

The doctrine of consideration was clarified in subsequent cases in England and the British colonies, including the United States. Today, we can identify the following elements of consideration:

1. A document not under seal requires consideration.
2. Consideration requires a benefit to the promisor or a detriment to the promise.
3. Moral consideration is insufficient (discussed further below).
4. The consideration must be induced by the promise.
5. The adequacy (amount) of the consideration is irrelevant.[26]

Most common law countries follow these same basic elements of consideration. However, courts have, in some limited instances, recognized moral obligations as valid consideration. In a 1782 case, Lord Mansfield found moral consideration to be sufficient to enforce a variety of promises, including the promise to pay a debt discharged by bankruptcy or barred by the statute of limitations, for instance.[27] However, this approach was rejected by British courts in later cases, such as *Eastwood v. Kenyon*, where a promise to pay a debt absent consideration was found to be unenforceable.[28]

Today, moral obligations are not valid consideration in most cases within common law courts. In the United States, courts have carved out a small cadre of exceptions, including an adult's promise to pay the debt of a minor; the promise to pay a debt that has been discharged due to bankruptcy or barred by the statute of limitations;[29] and a promise in which the promisor receives a material benefit and promises to pay out of moral obligation.[30] In most other cases, moral obligations are unenforceable in common law courts.

Despite the argument that *causa* cannot be compared to consideration due to structural and doctrinal differences between the two systems,[31] scholars continue to analogize the two.[32] Arguably the reasoning for the analogy stems from the fact that the requirement of consideration refuses to enforce gratuitous promises or contracts with third-party beneficiaries, while having *causa* can support such gratuitous promises and third-party beneficiaries.[33] With this in mind, both doctrines can be seen as an attempt to draw a line between enforceable and unenforceable contracts, with *causa* drawing more of a theoretical rule as opposed to a hard, practical rule like bargained-for-exchange.[34]

One scholar's reason for this distinction refers back again to the underlying premise of consent in civil law contracts and "the moral principle that contracts should be observed," contrasted with a "medieval system of common law writs that began with a decidedly restrictive view of enforceable obligations."[35] Scholar Julian Hermida argued that this underlying distinction would make the two concepts incomparable and that each doctrine is trying to solve its own problem.[36] While both may draw some line, Hermida argues that *causa* "aims at reflecting Aristotle's distinction between liberality and commutative justice," while consideration is "merely concerned about limiting in practice the promises that could be enforced."[37]

Whether the doctrines are comparable or too distinct, the underlying analogy behind the comparison is that both doctrines attempt to provide the "reason that justifies the assumed obligation."[38] Going further, one might argue that the "reason" is not necessarily *causa* or the contract's motive but consent in civil law and getting the benefit of the bargain in common law. From the earliest of comparative scholars, it was noted that the idea of *causa* was hard to describe as one particular thing because it applied in many contexts.[39] Perhaps due to its theoretical nature, early U.S. scholars deemed *causa* as "serv[ing] no proper object" because of its lack of a definite and precise meaning.[40]

Unlike the common law, the civil law places special emphasis on the categorization and classification of contracts.[41] The civil law code that dictates which contracts will be enforced is often divided into the "general law of contracts" (*lex generalis*) and the special law of individual contract (*lex specialis*).[42] Further, legal scholars (who are seen as "dominant actors of the civil law")[43] have divided contracts into more refined categories such as "nominated and innominate, consensual and real, bilateral and unilateral, and commutative and aleatory, among others."[44] Each type is said to have its own "legal nature."[45] Some of the categories are familiar in common law systems, but their definitions are different. In contrast, the common law has established formation principles that apply to all contracts with equitable exceptions.

The common law appears more concerned with distinction as opposed to classification, as seen in the courts of law versus equity and the contract versus the quasi-contract (promissory estoppel/reliance).[46] There are challenges in trying to compare one system to the other. Saying that consideration isn't required in civil law countries is true but misleading. The relevant Code will dictate what is required for contract validity in the civil law country. Determining whether a contract has a *causa* might force the lawyer to classify the contract at hand.[47] If the contract is bilateral or onerous, then *causa* takes the form of "receiving the equivalent of what one gave up," which, semantics aside, is very similar to the bargained-for-exchange definition of consideration.[48] The similarities and distinctions of the two systems may go on *ad infinitum* as the two continue to change over time. Understanding what contracts are valid and legally enforceable will require the lawyer to understand the most important similarities and differences between not just the contract law, but the legal system as a whole.

Is the common law approach workable for commercial contracts? Though the civil law approach codified in the 19th century is clear and enforces a broader array of contracts than the common law, the civil system is rigid and difficult to change in light of the creation of new forms of contracts (e.g., online contracts, franchise agreements, shrink wrap agreements). The common law, to the contrary, is flexible and constantly evolving to meet the demands of parties.

In the common law, "[e]very new case is an experiment ... The principles themselves are continually retested; for if the rules derived from a principle do not work well, the principle itself must ultimately be reexamined."[49] In the next section, I will examine the application of consideration in common law jurisdictions.

Notes

1 Arthur T. Von Mehren, *The French Civil Code and Contract: A Comparative Analysis of Contract Formation and Form*, 15 Louis. L. Rev. 687, 699–701 (1955).

2 *Bouvier's Law Dictionary* (1856 edition).

3 "The wager of law, if it ever had a legal existence in the United States, is now completely abolished." *Childress v. Emory*, 21 U.S. 8 (1823).

4 *Slade v. Morley*, 4 Co. Rep. 92b (1602) (emphasis added).

5 Von Mehren, supra note 1, at 700–702.

6 *Bouvier's Law Dictionary* (1856 edition).

7 James Gordley, *Louisiana and the Common Law: Le Jour de Gloire, Est-II Passe?*, 24 Tul. Eur. & Civ. L.F. 191 (2009); Caslav Pejovic, *Civil Law and Common Law: Two Different paths Leading to the Same Goal*, 32 VUWLR 817 (2001); Ernest G. Lorenzen, *Causa and Consideration in the Law of Contracts*, 28 Yale L.J. 621 (1919).

8 Charles R. Calleros, *Introducing Civil Law Students to Common Law Legal Method Through Contract Law*, 60 J. Legal Educ. 641, 650 (2010–2011).

9 John Henry Merryman and Rogelio Perez-Perdomo, *The Civil Law Tradition: An Introduction to the Legal Systems of Europe and Latin America* 24 (3d ed. 2007).

10 Calleros, supra note 8, at footnote 13.

> The German scholar Savigny doubted that a code could comprehensively anticipate "every case that may arise," because "there are positively no limits to the varieties of actual combinations of circumstances." Frederick

Charles von Savigny, Of the Vocation of Our Age for Legislation and Jurisprudence 38 (Abraham Hayward transl., The Legal Classics Library 1986). Nonetheless, Savigny cleverly used an example from geometry to describe the technique that judges might use to apply code provision and underlying principle to resolve any dispute; "In every triangle . . . there are certain data, from the relations of which all the rest are necessarily deductible: thus, given two sides and the included angle the while triangle is given. In like manner, every part of our law has points by which the rest may be given: these may be termed the leading axioms." Id. at 38–39.

11 Id. at 651 (citing Article 1108 of the French Code Civil).

12 To illustrate a barrier in comparing the two legal systems, the French law is to be interpreted in the strictest sense, whereas the common law incorporates the doctrines of stare decisis and precedent to determine the law's meaning. Id. at 642. Meanwhile, in the French system, the Cour de Cassation (the highest court, also called the court of last resort of civil obligations) can ignore prior rulings and a lower court can ignore a higher court's decision. Id. Another example can be seen in the Italian Civil Code of 1942, which provides that:

> In interpreting the statute, no other meaning can be attributed to it than that made clear by the actual significance of the words according to the connection between them, and by the intention of the legislature.

If a controversy cannot be decided by a precise provision, consideration is given to provisions that regulate similar cases or analogous matters; if the case still remains in doubt, it is decided according to general principles of the legal order of the State.

Merryman, supra note 9, at 44. The Code itself provides the interpretive framework, and, similar to many civil law countries, relies heavily on the provision's language itself and legislative intent. Id. If something remains unclear, as a last resort, the court is to refer to the "legal order of the State," which echoes to the notions of natural law that today's common law system has drifted far away from. Id. at 45. While in practice civil law countries have turned away from natural law and do get influenced by prior judicial decisions, the Code and the dominant judicial theories echo to notions the common law is essentially distinct from. Id. at 45–47. The interpretive differences also raise another key difference by inferring that the civil law, being legislation bound, may be slower to change than the common law.

13 Merryman, supra note 4, at 33.

14 Calleros, supra note 8, at 651 (citing Article 1108 of the French Code Civil) (translation done by Google).

15 Gordley, supra note 7, at 192.

16 Id.

17 Id. at 192, 205.

18 Julian Hermida, *Convergence of Civil Law and Common Law Contracts in the Space Field*, 34 Hong Kong L.J. 339, *14 (2004) (page number denotes page number of article as it was found at www.julianhermida.com/dossier/dossierpubhk.pdf).

19 Id. at *10.

20 Id.
21 Hermida, supra note 18, at *12 (comparing the general theory premised on a negative analysis of will to Louisiana and Argentina, where both countries require "that the consent must be given in the form of offers or proposals from one party to the other, which must be accepted by the other . . . in a way that resembles US common law contract theory.")
22 *Pillans v. Van Mierop*, 3 Burr. 1662 (1765).
23 *Pillans v. Van Mierop*, 3 Burr. 1663, 97 Eng. Rep. 1035 (K.B. 1765) (quoting from Lord Mansfield).
24 7 T.R. 350n, 101 Eng. Rep. 1014n (1778).
25 Id.
26 See Ernest G. Lorenzen, *Causa and Consideration in the Law of Contracts*, 7 Yale L.J. 42 (1919).
27 *Hawkes v. Saunders*, 1 Cowp. 289 (K.B. 1782).
28 11 Ad&E 438 (Q.B. 1840).
29 *Mills v. Wyman*, 20 Mass. (3 Pick.) 207 (1825) (moral obligation to pay for the gratuitous care of promisor's dying son found to be insufficient consideration).
30 *Webb v. McGowin*, 27 Ala. App. 82 (1935).
31 Id. at 14.
32 See, e.g., Calleros, supra note 8, at 651–653; Gordley, supra note 7, at 193; Pejovic, supra note 7, at 821–822.
33 Pejovic, supra note 7, at 822.
34 Calleros, supra note 8, at 651.
35 Id. at 653 (describing the concept as cause/causa as "expansive" and reflecting the "Napoleonic Code Civil's respect for the autonomy of the parties").
36 Hermida, supra note 18, at *14–15.
37 Id.
38 Id. at *14.
39 Lorenzen, supra note 7, at 646 ("There is in reality no definable 'doctrine' of causa. The term 'causa' includes a variety of notions which may equally well be derived from the nature of a juristic act and from considerations of equity.") (notably framed in terms of "law" and "equity").
40 Hermida, supra note 18, at *14.
41 Id. at *6.
42 Id. at *7.
43 Merryman, supra note 9, at 60.
44 Hermida, supra note 18, at *7.
45 Id.
46 This is opinion only.
47 Causa will likely be presumed and it is up to the party disputing the contract to prove its non-existence. See Hermida, supra note 18, at *15.
48 See, e.g., Id. at *15; Gordley, supra note 7, at 192, 205.
49 Munroe Smith, *Jurisprudence* 21 (1909).

3

THE JUDGE VS. THE LEGISLATURE

Cases and Statutes

Where does law come from? That question can be answered in different ways depending on what we mean by the word "law." In a civil law jurisdiction, the law refers to the statutes enacted by the legislature and the decrees and orders promulgated by ministries in accordance with those statutes. The same could be said of some law in the United States—the federal Congress or state legislative bodies pass statutes, which are signed into law by the president (federal) or governor (state). Executive agencies apply these laws through the issuance of regulations, which derive practical guidance from the broad outlines of the statutes.

Yet in the United States, there is an additional source of law—the courts. While a civil law judge might issue a written opinion that influences subsequent judgments, a common law judge's opinion creates binding law that ties the hands of judges in subsequent cases. In this way, the common law judge is creating "law" that has the same weight as a statute passed by the legislature. Accordingly, judges in the United States play a very important role in the creation of law.

I am often asked when I lecture, "Who is more powerful, the legislature or the courts?" That is a difficult question to answer. The legislature, just as in civil law countries, has the power to establish new laws from whole cloth. As the elected representatives of the people, it is their job to determine which laws are necessary and how to craft them. So long as they have majority support and executive concurrence, legislators have free rein to establish the laws that they see fit for their constituents. Once this process is done (and no sooner), the power shifts to the judicial branch. Upon the initiation of a case, the judicial branch has an opportunity to examine the law and to determine whether it is constitutional and whether it should stand as written, be modified, or be overturned.

In essence, all three branches of government—the legislative, executive, and judicial—are equally powerful. This was the intent of the founders, who wanted to create a system of governance that would divide power between different governing bodies so that the risk of tyranny would be diminished. While the legislature and executive largely rely on each other to act and face consequences for acting alone, the judicial branch stands ready to extinguish any actions that they deem to be against the intent of the Constitution. But it wasn't always this way.

The Judicial Power

The first three Articles of the U.S. Constitution create the three branches of government. The first two clearly stipulate the powers that the Executive and Legislative branches have. But the third Article is much less clear about the role of the Judiciary. Let's examine the three sections of that Article.

Section 1

The judicial power of the United States, shall be vested in one Supreme Court, and in such inferior courts as the Congress may from time to time ordain and establish. The judges, both of the supreme and inferior courts, shall hold their offices during good behaviour, and shall, at stated times, receive for their services, a compensation, which shall not be diminished during their continuance in office.

This section is rather straightforward. It creates the U.S. Supreme Court, the highest federal court in the country, and says that the Congress is free to create additional courts as necessary (which they did). In effect, this gives Congress an additional power (to create courts). All inferior courts created by Congress under this Article, including federal circuit courts and federal district courts, are known as "Article III Courts." Congress also has the power to create courts that handle non-judicial matters, such as tax and bankruptcy. These are known as "Article I Courts," and their decisions are subject to review by Article III Courts.

Section 2

The judicial power shall extend to all cases, in law and equity, arising under this Constitution, the laws of the United States, and treaties made, or which shall be made, under their authority;—to all cases affecting ambassadors, other public ministers and consuls;—to all cases of admiralty and maritime jurisdiction;—to controversies to which the United States shall be a party;—to controversies between two or more states;—between a state and citizens of another state;—between citizens of different states;—between citizens of the same state claiming lands under grants of different states, and between a state, or the citizens thereof, and foreign states, citizens or subjects.

In all cases affecting ambassadors, other public ministers and consuls, and those in which a state shall be party, the Supreme Court shall have original jurisdiction. In all the other cases before mentioned, the Supreme Court shall have appellate jurisdiction, both as to law and fact, with such exceptions, and under such regulations as the Congress shall make.

The trial of all crimes, except in cases of impeachment, shall be by jury; and such trial shall be held in the state where the said crimes shall have been committed; but when not committed within any state, the trial shall be at such place or places as the Congress may by law have directed.

Section 2 of this Article is more precise. The first clause establishes the range of cases that Article III Courts have competence to hear. The types of cases mentioned here include:

- All cases dealing with constitutional issues, federal statutes or treaties
- All cases affecting Ambassadors and other public officials

- All cases of admiralty and maritime law
- All cases where the United States is a party
- All cases between citizens of different states or countries

The second clause divides the courts' jurisdiction into "original" and "appellate." Original jurisdiction means that a case can go directly to the U.S. Supreme Court without working its way through the lower courts first. Only cases involving public officials or states have this fast-track access. All other cases mentioned above must be appealed from lower courts before being considered by the Supreme Court.

The final clause of this section establishes a right to a jury for all federal crimes except impeachment. The jury issue was extended to some civil cases by the Seventh Amendment to the U.S. Constitution.

Section 3

Treason against the United States, shall consist only in levying war against them, or in adhering to their enemies, giving them aid and comfort. No person shall be convicted of treason unless on the testimony of two witnesses to the same overt act, or on confession in open court.

The Congress shall have power to declare the punishment of treason, but no attainder of treason shall work corruption of blood, or forfeiture except during the life of the person attainted.

The final section of this Article clarifies the crime of treason, which shall only be defined to include declaring war against the United States or supporting enemies of the state.

What you should have noticed after reviewing the entirety of this Article is that it doesn't specify the power of the Judiciary in relation to the other branches of government. Nowhere does it set forth that the courts can overturn statutes or override executive action. Yet it is quite clearly established today that this power exists. This power comes from the Supreme Court itself, which felt obliged to interpret Article III only 15 years after the Constitution was ratified.

In *Marbury v. Madison*, one of the most famous constitutional law cases of all time in the United States, a dispute arose over the power of the Congress to reinterpret the nature of "original jurisdiction" for the Supreme Court to include authority to issue writs of mandamus. Though a seemingly small controversy, the justices of the Court took this as an opportunity to consider the scope of their power and their position among the branches of government.

The controversy began when outgoing President John Adams made numerous last-minute appointments of federal judges in an effort to ensure that his principles would continue to be protected after incoming President Thomas Jefferson, who hailed from a different political party, took office. The Court explained the process for commissioning magistrate judges, to which Mr. William Marbury had been appointed by President Adams:

> *The President of the United States, by signing the commission, appointed Mr. Marbury a justice of the peace for the County of Washington, in the District of Columbia, and the seal of the United States, affixed thereto by the Secretary of State, is conclusive testimony of the verity of the signature, and of the completion of the appointment; and the appointment conferred on him a legal right to the office for the space of five years. Having this legal right to the office, he has a consequent right to the commission, a refusal to deliver which is a plain violation of that right for which the laws of the country afford him a remedy.*

The last sentence of this paragraph highlights the problem that led to the lawsuit—Mr. Adams's Secretary of State, John Marshall (who had recently been appointed Chief Justice of the Supreme Court as well) was unable to complete the physical delivery of the commissions before President Jefferson took over. When Jefferson came to power, he immediately ordered the undelivered commissions to be cancelled. Marbury, who never received his commission, asked the Supreme Court directly for a writ of mandamus, which is an order from the court to force someone to take a certain action. In this case, the writ would order the new Secretary of State under President Jefferson to deliver the commission to Marbury.

Chief Justice Marshall quickly determined that Marbury was entitled to the commission and that the failure to deliver it to him physically did not necessarily void the commission. They also conclude that the writ of mandamus is the proper remedy in a case like this:

> *Where a commission to a public officer has been made out, signed, and sealed, and is withheld from the person entitled to it, an action of detinue for the commission against the Secretary of State who refuses to deliver it is not the proper remedy, as the judgment in detinue is for the thing itself, or its value. The value of a public office, not to be sold, is incapable of being ascertained. It is a plain case for a mandamus, either to deliver the commission or a copy of it from the record.*
>
> *Should the commission, instead of being evidence of an appointment, even be considered as constituting the appointment itself, still it would be made when the last act to be done by the President was performed, or, at furthest, when the commission was complete.*
>
> *The last act to be done by the President is the signature of the commission. He has then acted on the advice and consent of the Senate to his own nomination. The time for deliberation has then passed. He has decided. His judgment, on the advice and consent of the Senate concurring with his nomination, has been made, and the officer is appointed. This appointment is evidenced by an open, unequivocal act, and, being the last act required from the person making it, necessarily excludes the idea of its being, so far as it respects the appointment, an inchoate and incomplete transaction.*
>
> *It is then the opinion of the Court:*
>
> 1. *That, by signing the commission of Mr. Marbury, the President of the United States appointed him a justice of peace for the County of Washington in the District of Columbia, and that the seal of the United States, affixed thereto by the Secretary of State,*

is conclusive testimony of the verity of the signature, and of the completion of the appointment, and that the appointment conferred on him a legal right to the office for the space of five years.

2. *That, having this legal title to the office, he has a consequent right to the commission, a refusal to deliver which is a plain violation of that right, for which the laws of his country afford him a remedy.*[1]

Things appeared to be going well for Mr. Marbury at that point. However, the court then began its introspective process and began to analyze whether it had the power to issue such writs or whether Mr. Marbury had to first go through the lower courts and use the Supreme Court's appellate (rather than original) jurisdiction:

> *To enable the Court to issue a mandamus to compel the delivery of the commission of a public office by the Secretary of State, it must be shown that it is an exercise of appellate jurisdiction, or that it be necessary to enable them to exercise appellate jurisdiction.*
>
> *It is the essential criterion of appellate jurisdiction that it revises and corrects the proceedings in a cause already instituted, and does not create the cause.*
>
> *The authority given to the Supreme Court by the act establishing the judicial system of the United States to issue writs of mandamus to public officers appears not to be warranted by the Constitution.*
>
> *It is emphatically the duty of the Judicial Department to say what the law is. Those who apply the rule to particular cases must, of necessity, expound and interpret the rule. If two laws conflict with each other, the Court must decide on the operation of each.*
>
> *If courts are to regard the Constitution, and the Constitution is superior to any ordinary act of the legislature, the Constitution, and not such ordinary act, must govern the case to which they both apply.*

Chief Justice Marshall here is making it eminently clear that the Constitution is superior to any Act of Congress. Thus, when the legislature attempts to pass a law and that law conflicts with a provision of the Constitution, the law will be found unconstitutional. So what is the law that is problematic for the court here? It is the Judiciary Act of 1789, an Act passed by Congress that, among other things, "gave" the Supreme Court original jurisdiction over writs of mandamus.[2] This meant that parties could go directly to the Supreme Court with such requests rather than working their way through the lower courts first.

The problem was that the legislature was attempting to modify the Constitution by expanding the power of the Supreme Court, without following the Constitutional Amendment process outlined in that very document. The petitioners argued that the language of Article III was general and thus can be interpreted as open to adding new powers.

> *It has been insisted at the bar, that, as the original grant of jurisdiction to the Supreme and inferior courts is general, and the clause assigning original jurisdiction to the Supreme Court contains no negative or restrictive words, the power remains to the Legislature to assign original jurisdiction to that Court in other cases than those specified in the article which has been recited, provided those cases belong to the judicial power of the United States.*
>
> *If it had been intended to leave it in the discretion of the Legislature to apportion the judicial power between the Supreme and inferior courts according to the will of that body, it would certainly have been useless to have proceeded further than to have defined the judicial power and the tribunals in which it should be vested. The subsequent part of the section is mere surplusage—is entirely without meaning—if such is to be the construction.* If Congress remains at liberty to give this court appellate jurisdiction where the Constitution has declared their jurisdiction shall be original, and original jurisdiction where the Constitution has declared it shall be appellate, the distribution of jurisdiction made in the Constitution, is form without substance.
>
> *Affirmative words are often, in their operation, negative of other objects than those affirmed, and, in this case, a negative or exclusive sense must be given to them or they have no operation at all.*

It cannot be presumed that any clause in the Constitution is intended to be without effect, and therefore such construction is inadmissible unless the words require it.[3]

The Supreme Court concluded that the Judiciary Act of 1789, which expanded the court's original jurisdiction to include writs of mandamus, was unconstitutional. But whose role is it to interpret the meaning of the Constitution and to declare statutes void if they conflict with that document? This is where Justice Marshall spoke in no uncertain terms about the role of the Supreme Court:

It is emphatically the province and duty of the Judicial Department to say what the law is. Those who apply the rule to particular cases must, of necessity, expound and interpret that rule. If two laws conflict with each other, the Courts must decide on the operation of each.

So, if a law be in opposition to the Constitution, if both the law and the Constitution apply to a particular case, so that the Court must either decide that case conformably to the law, disregarding the Constitution, or conformably to the Constitution, disregarding the law, the Court must determine which of these conflicting rules governs the case. This is of the very essence of judicial duty.[4]

These words left no doubt that the Court had adopted the power of "judicial review," the power to examine acts of Congress or the president and to determine if they conform to the Court's interpretation of the Constitution. President Jefferson lashed out at Justice Marshall after this opinion was issued, claiming that the Court had effectively appointed itself the ultimate decision-maker over the validity of any congressional act:

You seem to consider the judges as the ultimate arbiters of all constitutional questions; a very dangerous doctrine indeed, and one which would place us under the despotism of an oligarchy. Our judges are as honest as other men, and not more so. They have,

> *with others, the same passions for party, for power, and the privilege of their corps. . . . Their power [is] the more dangerous as they are in office for life, and not responsible, as the other functionaries are, to the elective control. The Constitution has erected no such single tribunal, knowing that to whatever hands confided, with the corruptions of time and party, its members would become despots. It has more wisely made all the departments co-equal and co-sovereign within themselves.*[5]

This case ushered in a new era in American governance—one in which each branch of government had a significant and powerful role to play in the creation of law. Statutes became subservient to the interpretations of the courts and the courts became gatekeepers to the Constitution. Judicial review meant that both state and federal legislatures would always be under the watchful eye of the courts. Individuals who believed that the legislature was violating the Constitution had access to the courts to protect their rights, because "[t]he judicial power of the United States is extended to all cases arising under the Constitution."[6]

Evolving Opinions

Now that you understand how judicial review came to be, you may be wondering how this plays a role in legal analysis. The answer to that question is rooted in the Constitution. Consider the importance of size for a moment—bigger is not always better. The longest constitution in the world belongs to India, with 448 Articles.[7] It should be noted that there is a longer constitution out there, but not of a country. The state of Alabama has over 850 amendments to its 1901 constitution, making it the longest state constitution in the world.[8] The shortest? The United States Constitution, with 7 Articles and 27 amendments.

The reason that size matters in the context of legal analysis is that a longer constitution, even from a common law country like India, leaves little room for interpretation. Most civil law countries follow India's example and do their best to be comprehensive.[9] This approach provides clarity, predictability, and consistency in the promulgation of the law. Assuming citizens have read their constitutions, they should have a good sense of their rights. But can the same be said of citizens in the United States? For instance, how might you interpret the following Constitutional provision:

> *A well regulated militia, being necessary to the security of a free state, the right of the people to keep and bear arms, shall not be infringed.*[10]

That is the full text of the Second Amendment. What does it mean to you? Does it mean that the government can raise an army and that the army can have weapons? Or does it mean that citizens who are not necessarily part of the army can own guns? If you believe the latter interpretation to be correct, what is meant by "arms"? In 1791, when this Amendment was adopted as part of the Bill of Rights, the most dangerous arm was likely a musket that could fire one shot before undergoing a lengthy reloading process. Today, much more dangerous "arms" exist that could kill large groups of people quickly. Are those arms protected as well?

The St. Valentine's Day massacre occurred in 1929, in which Al Capone's Chicago-based mob allegedly massacred six rival gang members using short-barreled rifles and shotguns. In response, the federal government passed the 1934 National Firearms Act, which required all weapons not traditionally used by the militia to be registered and taxed with the agency that became the Alcohol, Tobacco and Firearms agency. Two individuals were charged with violating this law and they challenged its constitutionality. The case made its way to the U.S. Supreme Court in 1939, and the court concluded that the Act did not violate the Second Amendment since it was limited in application to weapons not used by the militia.[11]

While seemingly a victory for gun control activists, the court's language left a big door open for future cases. By insinuating that regulation of guns was permissible so long as those guns were not used by the military, gun rights advocates could argue that any weapon used by the military could not be regulated. As the military grew dramatically and expanded the types of weapons that it used, the 1939 decision paved the way to a broad array of arms access.

This trend was confirmed in the 2008 Supreme Court case of *District of Columbia v. Heller.*[12] In that case, Washington, D.C., had passed a law in 1975 that prevented ownership of handguns and that required registered shotguns and rifles to be kept unloaded in the home.[13] Six plaintiffs that wished to keep handguns in their home for self-defense and to keep their long guns loaded and ready to shoot intruders sued the District to challenge the constitutionality of the statute. The U.S. Supreme Court interpreted the Second Amendment to broadly protect an individual's right to bear arms, even if unconnected to military service. They noted that states could block related acts, such as carrying concealed weapons or carrying weapons near schools, but any statute that restricts the general right to bear arms would be unconstitutional. Note that this was a close decision (5–4) and is likely to be challenged in the future.

What we can learn from this example is that a short constitution places a great deal of power in the hands of the courts to explain what rights the citizens have and when those rights have been violated. It also shows how these rights can change over time and how the court can adapt its interpretation to fit the will of society at the time. But does this mean that the court is not bound to follow its past decisions? To answer this question, let's look at another example from the caselaw.

Consider a dark period in American history—the late 19th century. Slavery had just been abolished by President Abraham Lincoln,[14] and the Constitution was amended to give African Americans the right to equal protection of the laws shortly thereafter.[15] But these actions were not enough to quench the appetite in the Southern United States for discrimination.

The state of Louisiana in the American South enacted the Separate Car Act in 1890, which forced railroads to provide separate railcars for black and white passengers. Though the railway companies disagreed with the Act on the grounds of the additional expense involved, they complied with the law. In 1892, a "test case" was set in motion whereby a group of citizens that disagreed with the law planned to violate the law in order to challenge its constitutionality.

Courts in the United States are reactive, acting only when a person or group is injured by a law and thereafter challenges that law, not before. The constitutionality of a law thus cannot be challenged where the law has caused no injury.

The test case involved Mr. Homer Adolph Plessy, a man who appeared mostly white but for a black ancestor, making him mixed-race, which constituted "black" under Louisiana law. Mr. Plessy boarded the train car for white passengers only. He was duly arrested (by a detective hired by the group of citizens) and detained. He sued the state of Louisiana claiming that his Thirteenth and Fourteenth Amendment rights were violated by the Separate Car Act because his reputation was negatively impacted (taken away) by forcing him to ride in a separate car. The opinion is below. As you read it, consider the historical period in which it was written and how that shaped the opinion of the justices.

Plessy v. Ferguson[16]

MR. JUSTICE BROWN, after stating the case, delivered the opinion of the court.

This case turns upon the constitutionality of an act of the General Assembly of the State of Louisiana, passed in 1890, providing for separate railway carriages for the white and colored races.

The first section of the statute enacts "that all railway companies carrying passengers in their coaches in this State shall provide equal but separate accommodations for the white and colored races by providing two or more passenger coaches for each passenger train, or by dividing the passenger coaches by a partition so as to secure separate accommodations: Provided, That this section shall not be construed to apply to street railroads. No person or persons, shall be admitted to occupy seats in coaches other than the ones assigned to them on account of the race they belong to."

By the second section, it was enacted "that the officers of such passenger trains shall have power and are hereby required to assign each passenger to the coach or compartment used for the race to which such passenger belongs; any passenger insisting on going into a coach or compartment to which by race he does not belong shall be liable to a fine of twenty-five dollars, or in lieu thereof to imprisonment for a period of not more than twenty days in the parish prison, and any officer of any railroad insisting on assigning a passenger to a coach or compartment other than the one set aside for the race to which said passenger belongs shall be liable to a fine of twenty-five dollars, or in lieu thereof to imprisonment for a period of not more than twenty days in the parish prison; and should any passenger refuse to occupy the coach or compartment to which he or she is assigned by the officer of such railway, said officer shall have power to refuse to carry such passenger on his train, and for such refusal neither he nor the railway company which he represents shall be liable for damages in any of the courts of this State."

The third section provides penalties for the refusal or neglect of the officers, directors, conductors, and employees of railway companies to comply with the act, with a proviso that "nothing in this act shall be construed as applying to nurses attending children of the other race." The fourth section is immaterial.

The information filed in the criminal District Court charged in substance that Plessy, being a passenger between two stations within the State of Louisiana, was assigned by officers of the company to the coach used for the race to which he belonged, but he insisted upon going into a coach used by the race to which he did not belong. Neither in the information nor plea was his particular race or color averred. The petition for the writ of prohibition averred that petitioner was seven-eighths Caucasian and one eighth African blood; that the mixture of colored blood was not discernible in him, and that he was entitled to every right, privilege and immunity secured to citizens of the United States of the white race; and that, upon such theory, he took possession of a vacant seat in a coach where passengers of the white race were accommodated, and was ordered by the conductor to vacate said coach and take a seat in another assigned to persons of the colored race, and, having refused to comply with such demand, he was forcibly ejected with the aid of a police officer, and imprisoned in the parish jail to answer a charge of having violated the above act.

The constitutionality of this act is attacked upon the ground that it conflicts both with the Thirteenth Amendment of the Constitution, abolishing slavery, and the Fourteenth Amendment, which prohibits certain restrictive legislation on the part of the States.

1. *That it does not conflict with the Thirteenth Amendment, which abolished slavery and involuntary servitude, except as a punishment for crime, is too clear for argument. Slavery implies involuntary servitude—a state of bondage; the ownership of mankind as a chattel, or at least the control of the labor and services of one man for the benefit of another, and the absence of a legal right to the disposal of his own person, property and services. This amendment was said in the Slaughterhouse Cases, 16 Wall. 36, to have been intended primarily to abolish slavery as it had been previously known in this country, and that it equally forbade Mexican peonage or the Chinese coolie trade when they amounted to slavery or involuntary servitude, and that the use of the word "servitude" was intended to prohibit the use of all forms of involuntary slavery, of whatever class or name. It was intimated, however, in that case that this amendment was regarded by the statesmen of that day as insufficient to protect the colored race from certain laws which had been enacted in the Southern States, imposing upon the colored race onerous disabilities and burdens and curtailing their rights in the pursuit of life, liberty and property to such an extent that their freedom*

was of little value; and that the Fourteenth Amendment was devised to meet this exigency.

So, too, in the Civil Rights Cases, 109 U.S. 3, 109 U.S. 24, it was said that the act of a mere individual, the owner of an inn, a public conveyance or place of amusement, refusing accommodations to colored people cannot be justly regarded as imposing any badge of slavery or servitude upon the applicant, but only as involving an ordinary civil injury, properly cognizable by the laws of the State and presumably subject to redress by those laws until the contrary appears. "It would be running the slavery argument into the ground," said Mr. Justice Bradley, "to make it apply to every act of discrimination which a person may see fit to make as to the guests he will entertain, or as to the people he will take into his coach or cab or car, or admit to his concert or theatre, or deal with in other matters of intercourse or business."

A statute which implies merely a legal distinction between the white and colored races—a distinction which is founded in the color of the two races and which must always exist so long as white men are distinguished from the other race by color—has no tendency to destroy the legal equality of the two races, or reestablish a state of involuntary servitude. Indeed, we do not understand that the Thirteenth Amendment is strenuously relied upon by the plaintiff in error in this connection.

By the Fourteenth Amendment, all persons born or naturalized in the United States and subject to the jurisdiction thereof are made citizens of the United States and of the State wherein they reside, and the States are forbidden from making or enforcing any law which shall abridge the privileges or immunities of citizens of the United States, or shall deprive any person of life, liberty, or property without due process of law, or deny to any person within their jurisdiction the equal protection of the laws.

The proper construction of this amendment was first called to the attention of this court in the Slaughterhouse Cases, 16 Wall. 36, which involved, however, not a question of race, but one of exclusive privileges. The case did not call for any expression of opinion as to the exact rights it was intended to secure to the colored race, but it was said generally that its main purpose was to establish the citizenship of the negro, to give definitions of citizenship of the United States and of the States, and to protect from the hostile legislation of the States the privileges and immunities of citizens of the United States, as distinguished from those of citizens of the States.

The object of the amendment was undoubtedly to enforce the absolute equality of the two races before the law, but, in the nature of things, it could not have been intended to abolish distinctions based upon color, or to enforce social, as distinguished from political, equality, or a commingling of the two races upon terms unsatisfactory to either. Laws permitting, and even requiring, their separation in places where they are liable to be brought into contact do not necessarily imply the inferiority of either race to the other, and have been generally, if not universally, recognized as within the competency of the state legislatures in the exercise of their police power. The most common instance of this is connected with the establishment of separate schools for white and colored children, which has been held to be a valid exercise of the legislative power even by courts of States where the political rights of the colored race have been longest and most earnestly enforced.

One of the earliest of these cases is that of Roberts v. City of Boston, *5 Cush. 19, in which the Supreme Judicial Court of Massachusetts held that the general school committee of Boston had power to make provision for the instruction of colored children in separate schools established exclusively for them, and to prohibit their attendance upon the other schools. "The great principle," said Chief Justice Shaw, p. 206, "advanced by the learned and eloquent advocate for the plaintiff" (Mr. Charles Sumner), "is that, by the constitution and laws of Massachusetts, all persons without distinction of age or sex, birth or color, origin or condition, are equal before the law. . . . But when this great principle comes to be applied to the actual and various conditions of persons in society, it will not warrant the assertion that men and women are legally clothed with the same civil and political powers, and that children and adults are legally to have the same functions and be subject to the same treatment, but only that the rights of all, as they are settled and regulated by law, are equally entitled to the paternal consideration and protection of the law for their maintenance and security."*

It was held that the powers of the committee extended to the establishment of separate schools for children of different ages, sexes and colors, and that they might also establish special schools for poor and neglected children, who have become too old to attend the primary school and yet have not acquired the rudiments of learning to enable them to enter the ordinary schools. Similar laws have been enacted by Congress under its general power of legislation over the District of Columbia, Rev.Stat.D.C. §§ 281, 282, 283, 310, 319, as well as by the legislatures of many of the States, and have been generally, if not uniformly, sustained by the courts. State v. McCann, *21 Ohio St. 198;* Lehew v. Brummell, *15 S.W.Rep. 765;* Ward v. Flood, *48 California 36;* Bertonneau v. School Directors, *3 Woods 177;* People v. Gallagher, *93 N.Y. 438;* Cory v. Carter, *48 Indiana 897;* Dawson v. Lee, *3 Kentucky 49.*

Laws forbidding the intermarriage of the two races may be said in a technical sense to interfere with the freedom of contract, and yet have been universally recognized as within the police power of the State. State v. Gibson, *36 Indiana 389.*

The distinction between laws interfering with the political equality of the negro and those requiring the separation of the two races in schools, theatres and railway carriages has been frequently drawn by this court. Thus, in Strauder v. West Virginia, *100 U.S. 303, it was held that a law of West Virginia limiting to white male persons, 21 years of age and citizens of the State, the right to sit upon juries was a discrimination which implied a legal inferiority in civil society, which lessened the security of the right of the colored race, and was a step toward reducing them to a condition of servility. Indeed, the right of a colored man that, in the selection of jurors to pass upon his life, liberty, and property, there shall be no exclusion of his race and no discrimination against them because of color has been asserted in a number of cases.* Virginia v. Rives, *100 U.S. 313;* Neal v. Delaware, *103 U.S. 370;* Bush v. Kentucky, *107 U.S. 110;* Gibson v. Mississippi, *162 U.S. 565. So, where the laws of a particular locality or the charter of a particular railway corporation has provided that no person shall be excluded from the cars on account of color, we have held that this meant that persons of color should travel in the same car as white ones, and that the enactment was not satisfied by the company's providing cars assigned exclusively to people of color, though they were as good as those which they assigned exclusively to white persons.* Railroad Company v. Brown, *17 Wall. 445.*

Upon the other hand, where a statute of Louisiana required those engaged in the transportation of passengers among the States to give to all persons traveling within that State, upon vessels employed in that business, equal rights and privileges in all parts of the vessel, without distinction on account of race or color, and subjected to an action for damages the owner of such a vessel, who excluded colored passengers on account of their color from the cabin set aside by him for the use of whites, it was held to be, so far as it applied to interstate commerce, unconstitutional and void. Hall v. De Cuir, *95 U.S. 48. The court in this case, however, expressly disclaimed that it had anything whatever to do with the statute as a regulation of internal commerce, or affecting anything else than commerce among the States.*

In the Civil Rights Case, 109 U.S. 3, it was held that an act of Congress entitling all persons within the jurisdiction of the United States to the full and equal enjoyment of the accommodations, advantages, facilities and privileges of inns, public conveyances, on land or water, theatres and other places of public amusement, and made applicable to citizens of every race and color, regardless of any previous condition of servitude, was unconstitutional and void upon the ground that the Fourteenth Amendment was prohibitory upon the States only, and the legislation authorized to be adopted by Congress for enforcing it was not direct legislation on matters respecting which the States were prohibited from making or enforcing certain laws, or doing certain acts, but was corrective legislation such as might be necessary or proper for counteracting and redressing the effect of such laws or acts. In delivering the opinion of the court, Mr. Justice Bradley observed that the Fourteenth Amendment "does not invest Congress with power to legislate upon subjects that are within the domain of state legislation, but to provide modes of relief against state legislation or state action of the kind referred to. It does not authorize Congress to create a code of municipal law for the regulation of private rights, but to provide modes of redress against the operation of state laws and the action of state officers, executive or judicial, when these are subversive of the fundamental rights specified in the amendment. Positive rights and privileges are undoubtedly secured by the Fourteenth Amendment, but they are secured by way of prohibition against state laws and state proceedings affecting those rights and privileges, and by power given to Congress to legislate for the purpose of carrying such prohibition into effect, and such legislation must necessarily be predicated upon such supposed state laws or state proceedings, and be directed to the correction of their operation and effect."

Much nearer, and, indeed, almost directly in point is the case of the Louisville, New Orleans &c. Railway v. Mississippi, *133 U.S. 587, wherein the railway company was indicted for a violation of a statute of Mississippi enacting that all railroads carrying passengers should provide equal but separate accommodations for the white and colored races by providing two or more passenger cars for each passenger train, or by dividing the passenger cars by a partition so as to secure separate accommodations. The case was presented in a different aspect from the one under consideration, inasmuch as it was an indictment against the railway company for failing to provide the separate accommodations, but the question considered was the constitutionality of the law. In that case, the Supreme Court of Mississippi, 66 Mississippi 662, had held that the statute applied solely to commerce within the State, and that, being the construction of the state statute by its highest court, was accepted as conclusive. "If it be a matter," said the court, p. 591, "respecting commerce wholly within a State, and not interfering with commerce between the States, then obviously there is no violation of the commerce clause of the Federal Constitution. . . . No question arises under this section as to the power of the State to separate in different compartments interstate passengers or affect in any manner the privileges and rights of such passengers. All that we can consider is whether the State has the power to require that railroad trains within her limits shall have separate accommodations for the two races; that affecting only commerce within the State is no invasion of the power given to Congress by the commerce clause."*

A like course of reasoning applies to the case under consideration, since the Supreme Court of Louisiana in the case of the State ex rel. Abbott v. Hicks, Judge, et al., *44 La.Ann. 770, held that the statute in question did not apply to interstate passengers, but was confined in its application to passengers traveling exclusively within the borders of the State. The case was decided largely upon the authority of* Railway Co. v. State, *66 Mississippi 662, and affirmed by this court in 133 U.S. 587. In the present case, no question of interference with interstate commerce can possibly arise, since the East Louisiana Railway appears to have been purely a local line, with both its termini within the State of Louisiana. Similar statutes for the separation of the to races upon public conveyances were held to be constitutional in* West Chester &c. Railroad v. Miles, *55 Penn.St. 209;* Day v. Owen, *5 Michigan 520;* Chicago &c. Railway v. Williams, *5 Illinois 185;* Chesapeake &c. Railroad v. Wells, *85 Tennessee 613;* Memphis &c. Railroad v. Benson, *85 Tennessee 627; The Sue, 22 Fed.Rep. 83;* Logwood v. Memphis &c. Railroad, *23 Fed.Rep. 318;* McGuinn v. Forbes, *37 Fed.Rep. 639;* People v. King, *18 N.E.Rep. 245;* Houck v. South Pac. Railway, *38 Fed.Rep. 226;* Heard v. Georgia Railroad Co., *3 Int. Com.Com'n 111; S.C., 1 Ibid. 428.*

While we think the enforced separation of the races, as applied to the internal commerce of the State, neither abridges the privileges or immunities of the colored man, deprives him of his property without due process of law, nor denies him the equal protection of the laws within the meaning of the Fourteenth Amendment, we are not prepared to say that the conductor, in assigning passengers to the coaches according to their race, does not act at his peril, or that the provision of the second section of the act that denies to the passenger compensation in damages for a refusal to receive him into the coach in which he properly belongs is a valid exercise of the legislative power. Indeed, we understand it to be conceded by the State's Attorney that such part of the act as exempts from liability the railway company and its officers is unconstitutional. The power to assign to a particular coach obviously implies the power to determine to which race the passenger belongs, as well as the power to determine who, under the laws of the particular State, is to be deemed a white and who a colored person. This question, though indicated in the brief of the plaintiff in error, does not properly arise upon the record in this case, since the only issue made is as to the unconstitutionality of the act so far as it requires the railway to provide separate accommodations and the conductor to assign passengers according to their race.

It is claimed by the plaintiff in error that, in any mixed community, the reputation of belonging to the dominant race, in this instance the white race, is property in the same sense that a right of action or of inheritance is property. Conceding this to be so for the purposes of this case, we are unable to see how this statute deprives him of, or in any way affects his right to, such property. If he be a white man and assigned to a colored coach, he may have his action for damages against the company for being deprived of his so-called property. Upon the other hand, if he be a colored man and be so assigned, he has been deprived of no property, since he is not lawfully entitled to the reputation of being a white man.

In this connection, it is also suggested by the learned counsel for the plaintiff in error that the same argument that will justify the state legislature in requiring railways to provide separate accommodations for the two races will also authorize them to require separate cars to be provided for people whose hair is of a certain color, or who are aliens, or who belong to certain nationalities, or to enact laws requiring colored people to walk upon one side of the street and white people upon the other, or requiring white men's houses to be painted white and colored men's black, or their vehicles or business signs to be of different colors, upon the theory that one side of the street is as good as the other, or that a house or vehicle of one color is as good as one of another color. The reply to all this is that every exercise of the police power must be reasonable, and extend only to such laws as are enacted in good faith for the promotion for the public good, and not for the annoyance or oppression of a particular class. Thus, in Yick Wo v. Hopkins, *118 U.S. 356, it was held by this court that a municipal ordinance of the city of San Francisco to regulate the carrying on of public laundries within the limits of the municipality violated the provisions of the Constitution of the United States if it conferred upon the municipal authorities arbitrary power, at their own will and without regard to discretion, in the legal sense of the term, to give or withhold consent as to persons or places without regard to the competency of the persons applying or the propriety of the places selected for the carrying on of the business. It was held to be a covert attempt on the part of the municipality to make an arbitrary and unjust discrimination against the Chinese race. While this was the case of a municipal ordinance, a like principle has been held to apply to acts of a state legislature passed in the exercise of the police power. Railroad Company v. Husen,* 95 U.S. 465; Louisville & Nashville Railroad v. Kentucky, *161 U.S. 677, and cases cited on p. 161 U.S. 700;* Duggett v. Hudson, *43 Ohio St. 548;* Capen v. Foster, *12 Pick. 48;* State ex rel. Wood v. Baker, *38 Wisconsin 71;* Monroe v. Collins, *17 Ohio St. 66;* Hulseman v. Rems, *41 Penn. St. 396;* Orman v. Riley, *1 California 48.*

So far, then, as a conflict with the Fourteenth Amendment is concerned, the case reduces itself to the question whether the statute of Louisiana is a reasonable regulation, and, with respect to this, there must necessarily be a large discretion on the part of the legislature. In determining the question of reasonableness, it is at liberty to act with reference to the established usages, customs, and traditions of the people, and with a view to the promotion of their comfort and the preservation of the public peace and good order. Gauged by this standard, we cannot say that a law which authorizes or even requires the separation of the two races in public conveyances is unreasonable, or more obnoxious to the Fourteenth Amendment than the acts of Congress requiring separate schools for colored children in the District of Columbia, the constitutionality of which does not seem to have been questioned, or the corresponding acts of state legislatures.

We consider the underlying fallacy of the plaintiff's argument to consist in the assumption that the enforced separation of the two races stamps the colored race with a badge of inferiority. If this be so, it is not by reason of anything found in the act, but solely because the colored race chooses to put that construction upon it. The argument necessarily assumes that if, as has been more than once the case and is not unlikely to be so again, the colored race should become the dominant power in the state legislature, and should enact a law in precisely similar terms, it would thereby relegate the white race to an inferior position. We imagine that the white race, at least, would not acquiesce in this assumption. The argument also assumes that social prejudices may be overcome by legislation, and that equal rights cannot be secured to the negro except by an enforced commingling of the two races. We cannot accept this proposition. If the two races are to meet upon terms of social equality, it must be the result of natural affinities, a mutual appreciation of each other's merits, and a voluntary consent of individuals. As was said by the Court of Appeals of New York in People v. Gallagher, *93 N. Y. 438, 448, "this end can neither be accomplished nor promoted by laws which conflict with the general sentiment of the community upon whom they are designed to operate. When the government, therefore, has secured to each of its citizens equal rights before the law and equal opportunities for improvement and progress, it has accomplished the end for which it was organized, and performed all of the functions respecting social advantages with which it is endowed."*

Legislation is powerless to eradicate racial instincts or to abolish distinctions based upon physical differences, and the attempt to do so can only result in accentuating the difficulties of the present situation. If the civil and political rights of both races be equal, one cannot be inferior to the other civilly or politically. If one race be inferior to the other socially, the Constitution of the United States cannot put them upon the same plane.

It is true that the question of the proportion of colored blood necessary to constitute a colored person, as distinguished from a white person, is one upon which there is a difference of opinion in the different States, some holding that any visible admixture of black blood stamps the person as belonging to the colored race (State v. Chaver, *5 Jones [N.C.] 1, p. 11); others that it depends upon the preponderance of blood* (Gray v. State, *4 Ohio 354;* Monroe v. Collins, *17 Ohio St. 665); and still others that the predominance of white blood must only be in the proportion of three-fourths.* (People v. Dean, *4 Michigan 406;* Jones v. Commonwealth, *80 Virginia 538). But these are questions to be determined under the laws of each State, and are not properly put in issue in this case. Under the allegations of his petition, it may undoubtedly become a question of importance whether, under the laws of Louisiana, the petitioner belongs to the white or colored race.*

The judgment of the court below is, therefore,

Affirmed.

MR. JUSTICE HARLAN, dissenting.

By the Louisiana statute the validity of which is here involved, all railway companies (other than street railroad companies) carrying passengers in that State are required to have separate but equal accommodations for white and colored persons "by providing two or more passenger coaches for each passenger train, or by dividing the passenger coaches by a partition so as to secure separate accommodations."

Under this statute, no colored person is permitted to occupy a seat in a coach assigned to white persons, nor any white person to occupy a seat in a coach assigned to colored persons. The managers of the railroad are not allowed to exercise any discretion in the premises, but are required to assign each passenger to some coach or compartment set apart for the exclusive use of his race. If a passenger insists upon going into a coach or compartment not set apart for persons of his race, he is subject to be fined or to be imprisoned in the parish jail. Penalties are prescribed for the refusal or neglect of the officers, directors, conductors and employees of railroad companies to comply with the provisions of the act.

Only "nurses attending children of the other race "are excepted from the operation of the statute. No exception is made of colored attendants traveling with adults. A white man is not permitted to have his colored servant with him in the same coach, even if his condition of health requires the constant, personal assistance of such servant. If a colored maid insists upon riding in the same coach with a white woman whom she has been employed to serve, and who may need her personal attention while traveling, she is subject to be fined or imprisoned for such an exhibition of zeal in the discharge of duty.

While there may be in Louisiana persons of different races who are not citizens of the United States, the words in the act "white and colored races" necessarily include all citizens of the United States of both races residing in that State. So that we have before us a state enactment that compels, under penalties, the separation of the two races in railroad passenger coaches and makes it a crime for a citizen of either race to enter a coach that has been assigned to citizens of the other race.

Thus, the State regulates the use of a public highway by citizens of the United States solely upon the basis of race.

However apparent the injustice of such legislation may be, we have only to consider whether it is consistent with the Constitution of the United States.

That a railroad is a public highway, and that the corporation which owns or operates it is in the exercise of public functions, is not, at this day, to be disputed. Mr. Justice Nelson, speaking for this court in New Jersey Steam Navigation Co. v. Merchants' Bank, *6 How. 344, 47 U.S. 382, said that a common carrier was in the exercise "of a sort of public office, and has public duties to perform, from which he should not be permitted to exonerate himself without the assent of the parties concerned."*

Mr. Justice Strong, delivering the judgment of this court in Olcott v. The Supervisors, *16 Wall. 678, 83 U.S. 694, said:*

"That railroads, though constructed by private corporations and owned by them, are public highways has been the doctrine of nearly all the courts ever since such conveniences for passage and transportation have had any existence. Very early the question arose whether a State's right of eminent domain could be exercised by a private corporation created for the purpose of constructing a railroad. Clearly it could not unless taking land for such a purpose by such an agency is taking land for public use. The right of eminent domain nowhere justifies taking property for a private use. Yet it is a doctrine universally accepted that a state legislature may authorize a private corporation to take land for the construction of such a road, making compensation to the owner. What else does this doctrine mean if not that building a railroad, though it be built by a private corporation, is an act done for a public use."

So, in Township of Pine Grove v. Talcott, *19 Wall. 666, 86 U.S. 676: "Though the corporation [a railroad company] was private, its work was public, as much so as if it were to be constructed by the State." So, in* Inhabitants of Worcester v. Western Railroad Corporation, *4 Met. 564:*

"The establishment of that great thoroughfare is regarded as a public work, established by public authority, intended for the public use and benefit, the use of which is secured to the whole community, and constitutes, therefore, like a canal, turnpike or highway, a public easement. It is true that the real and personal property necessary to the establishment and management of the railroad is vested in the corporation, but it is in trust for the public."

In respect of civil rights common to all citizens, the Constitution of the United States does not, I think, permit any public authority to know the race of those entitled to be protected in the enjoyment of such rights. Every true man has pride of race, and, under appropriate circumstances, when the rights of others, his equals before the law, are not to be affected, it is his privilege to express such pride and to take such action based upon it as to him seems proper. But I deny that any legislative body or judicial tribunal may have regard to the race of citizens when the civil rights of those citizens are involved. Indeed, such legislation as that here in question is inconsistent not only with that equality of rights which pertains to citizenship, National and State, but with the personal liberty enjoyed by everyone within the United States.

The Thirteenth Amendment does not permit the withholding or the deprivation of any right necessarily inhering in freedom. It not only struck down the institution of slavery as previously existing in the United States, but it prevents the imposition of any burdens or disabilities that constitute badges of slavery or servitude. It decreed universal civil freedom in this country. This court has so adjudged. But that amendment having been found inadequate to the protection of the rights of those who had been in slavery, it was followed by the Fourteenth Amendment, which added greatly to the dignity and glory of American citizenship and to the security of personal liberty by declaring that "all persons born or naturalized in the United States, and subject to the jurisdiction thereof, are citizens of the United States and of the State wherein they reside," and that "no State shall make or enforce any law which shall abridge the privileges or immunities of citizens of the United States; nor shall any State deprive any person of life, liberty or property without due process of law, nor deny to any person within its jurisdiction the equal protection of the laws."

These two amendments, if enforced according to their true intent and meaning, will protect all the civil rights that pertain to freedom and citizenship. Finally, and to the end that no citizen should be denied, on account of his race, the privilege of participating in the political control of his country, it as declared by the

Fifteenth Amendment that "the right of citizens of the United States to vote shall not be denied or abridged by the United States or by any State on account of race, color or previous condition of servitude."

These notable additions to the fundamental law were welcomed by the friends of liberty throughout the world. They removed the race line from our governmental systems. They had, as this court has said, a common purpose, namely to secure "to a race recently emancipated, a race that through many generations have been held in slavery, all the civil rights that the superior race enjoy."

They declared, in legal effect, this court has further said,

"that the law in the States shall be the same for the black as for the white; that all persons, whether colored or white, shall stand equal before the laws of the States, and, in regard to the colored race, for whose protection the amendment was primarily designed, that no discrimination shall be made against them by law because of their color."

We also said:

"The words of the amendment, it is true, are prohibitory, but they contain a necessary implication of a positive immunity, or right, most valuable to the colored race—the right to exemption from unfriendly legislation against them distinctively as colored—exemption from legal discriminations, implying inferiority in civil society, Lessening the security of their enjoyment of the rights which others enjoy, and discriminations which are steps towards reducing them to the condition of a subject race."

It was, consequently, adjudged that a state law that excluded citizens of the colored race from juries, because of their race and however well qualified in other respects to discharge the duties of jurymen, was repugnant to the Fourteenth Amendment. Strauder v. West Virginia,*100 U.S. 303, 100 U.S. 306, 100 U.S. 307;* Virginia v. Rives,*100 U.S. 313; Ex parte Virginia,100 U.S. 339; Neal v. Delaware,103 U.S. 370, 103 U.S. 386;* Bush v. Kentucky, *107 U.S. 110, 107 U.S. 116. At the present term, referring to the previous adjudications, this court declared that "underlying all of those decisions is the principle that the Constitution of the United States, in its present form, forbids, so far as civil and political rights are concerned, discrimination by the General Government or the States against any citizen because of his race. All citizens are equal before the law."*

Gibson v. Mississippi, 162 U.S. 565.

The decisions referred to show the scope of the recent amendments of the Constitution. They also show that it is not within the power of a State to prohibit colored citizens, because of their race, from participating as jurors in the administration of justice.

It was said in argument that the statute of Louisiana does not discriminate against either race, but prescribes a rule applicable alike to white and colored citizens. But this argument does not meet the difficulty. Everyone knows that the statute in question had its origin in the purpose not so much to exclude white persons from railroad cars occupied by blacks as to exclude colored people from coaches occupied by or assigned to white persons. Railroad corporations of Louisiana did not make discrimination among whites in the matter of accommodation for travelers. The thing to accomplish was, under the guise of giving equal accommodation for whites and blacks, to compel the latter to keep to themselves while traveling in railroad passenger coaches. No one would be so wanting in candor as to assert the contrary. The fundamental objection, therefore, to the statute is that it interferes with the personal freedom of citizens. "Personal liberty," it has been well said,

*"consists in the power of locomotion, of changing situation, or removing one's person to whatsoever places one's own inclination may direct, without imprisonment or restraint unless by due course of law." 1 Bl.Com. *134. If a white man and a black man choose to occupy the same public conveyance on a public highway, it is their right to do so, and no government, proceeding alone on grounds of race, can prevent it without infringing the personal liberty of each.*

It is one thing for railroad carriers to furnish, or to be required by law to furnish, equal accommodations for all whom they are under a legal duty to carry. It is quite another thing for government to forbid citizens of the white and black races from traveling in the same public conveyance, and to punish officers of railroad companies for permitting persons of the two races to occupy the same passenger coach. If a State can prescribe, as a rule of civil conduct, that whites and blacks shall not travel as passengers in the same railroad coach, why may it not so regulate the use of the streets of its cities and towns as to compel white citizens to keep on one side of a street and black citizens to keep on the other? Why may it not, upon like grounds, punish whites and blacks who ride together in streetcars or in open vehicles on a public road or street? Why may it not require sheriffs to assign whites to one side of a courtroom and blacks to the other? And why may it not also prohibit the commingling of the two races in the galleries of legislative halls or in public assemblages convened for the consideration of the political questions of the day? Further, if this statute of Louisiana is consistent with the personal liberty of citizens, why may not the State require the separation in railroad coaches of native and naturalized citizens of the United States, or of Protestants and Roman Catholics?

The answer given at the argument to these questions was that regulations of the kind they suggest would be unreasonable, and could not, therefore, stand before the law. Is it meant that the determination of questions of legislative power depends upon the inquiry whether the statute whose validity is questioned is, in the judgment of the courts, a reasonable one, taking all the circumstances into consideration? A statute may be unreasonable merely because a sound public policy forbade its enactment. But I do not understand that the courts have anything to do with the policy or expediency of legislation. A statute may be valid and yet, upon grounds of public policy, may well be characterized as unreasonable. Mr. Sedgwick correctly states the rule when he says that, the legislative intention being clearly ascertained, "the courts have no other duty to perform than to execute the legislative will, without any regard to their views as to the wisdom or justice of the particular enactment." Stat. & Const. Constr. 324.

There is a dangerous tendency in these latter days to enlarge the functions of the courts by means of judicial interference with the will of the people as expressed by the legislature. Our institutions have the distinguishing characteristic that the three departments of government are coordinate and separate. Each must keep within the limits defined by the Constitution. And the courts best discharge their duty by executing the will of the lawmaking power, constitutionally expressed, leaving the results of legislation to be dealt with by the people through their representatives. Statutes must always have a reasonable construction. Sometimes they are to be construed strictly; sometimes liberally, in order to carry out the legislative will. But however construed, the intent of the legislature is to be respected, if the particular statute in question is valid, although the courts, looking at the public interests, may conceive the statute to be both unreasonable and impolitic. If the power exists to enact a statute, that ends the matter so far as the courts are concerned. The adjudged cases in which statutes have been held to be void because unreasonable are those in which the means employed by the legislature were not at all germane to the end to which the legislature was competent.

The white race deems itself to be the dominant race in this country. And so it is in prestige, in achievements, in education, in wealth and in power. So, I doubt not, it will continue to be for all time if it remains true to its great heritage and holds fast to the principles of constitutional liberty. But in view of the Constitution, in the eye of the law, there is in this country no superior, dominant, ruling class of citizens. There is no caste here. Our Constitution is color-blind, and neither knows nor tolerates classes among citizens. In respect of civil rights, all citizens are equal before the law. The humblest is the peer of the most powerful. The law regards man as man, and takes no account of his surroundings or of his color when his civil rights as guaranteed by the supreme law of the land are involved. It is therefore to be regretted that this high tribunal, the final expositor of the fundamental law of the land, has reached the conclusion that it is competent for a State to regulate the enjoyment by citizens of their civil rights solely upon the basis of race.

In my opinion, the judgment this day rendered will, in time, prove to be quite as pernicious as the decision made by this tribunal in the Dred Scott Case. It was adjudged in that case that the descendants of Africans who were imported into this country and sold as slaves were not included nor intended to be included under the word "citizens" in the Constitution, and could not claim any of the rights and privileges which that instrument provided for and secured to citizens of the United States; that, at the time of the adoption of the Constitution, they were "considered as a subordinate and inferior class of beings, who had been subjugated by the dominant race, and, whether emancipated or not, yet remained subject to their authority, and had no rights or privileges but such as those who held the power and the government might choose to grant them." 19 How. 60 U.S. 393, 60 U.S. 404. The recent amendments of the Constitution, it was supposed, had eradicated these principles from our institutions. But it seems that we have yet, in some of the States, a dominant race—a superior class of citizens, which assumes to regulate the enjoyment of civil rights, common to all citizens, upon the basis of race. The present decision, it may well be apprehended, will not only stimulate aggressions, more or less brutal and irritating, upon the admitted rights of colored citizens, but will encourage the belief that it is possible, by means of state enactments, to defeat the beneficent purposes which the people of the United States had in view when they adopted the recent amendments of the Constitution, by one of which the blacks of this country were made citizens of the United States and of the States in which they respectively reside, and whose privileges and immunities, as citizens, the States are forbidden to abridge. Sixty millions of whites are in no danger from the presence here of eight millions of blacks. The destinies of the two races in this country are indissolubly linked together, and the interests of both require that the common government of all shall not permit the seeds of race hate to be planted under the sanction of law. What can more certainly arouse race hate, what more certainly create and perpetuate a feeling of distrust between these races, than state enactments which, in fact, proceed on the ground that colored citizens are so inferior and degraded that they cannot be allowed to sit in public coaches occupied by white citizens. That, as all will admit, is the real meaning of such legislation as was enacted in Louisiana.

The sure guarantee of the peace and security of each race is the clear, distinct, unconditional recognition by our governments, National and State, of every right that inheres in civil freedom, and of the equality before the law of all citizens of the United States, without regard to race. State enactments regulating the enjoyment of civil rights upon the basis of race, and cunningly devised to defeat legitimate results of the war under the pretence of recognizing equality of rights, can have no other result than to render permanent peace impossible and to keep alive a conflict of races the continuance of which must do harm to all concerned. This question is not met by the suggestion that social equality cannot exist between the white and black races in this country. That argument, if it can be properly regarded as one, is scarcely worthy of consideration, for social equality no more exists between two races when traveling in a passenger coach or a public highway than when members of the same races sit by each other in a street car or in the jury box, or stand or sit with each other in a political assembly, or when they use in common the street of a city or town, or when they are in the same room for the purpose of having their names placed on the registry of voters, or when they approach the ballot box in order to exercise the high privilege of voting.

There is a race so different from our own that we do not permit those belonging to it to become citizens of the United States. Persons belonging to it are, with few exceptions, absolutely excluded from our country. I allude to the Chinese race. But, by the statute in question, a Chinaman can ride in the same passenger coach with white citizens of the United States, while citizens of the black race in Louisiana, many of whom, perhaps, risked their lives for the preservation of the Union, who are entitled, by law, to participate in the political control of the State and nation, who are not excluded, by law or by reason of their race, from public stations of any kind, and who have all the legal rights that belong to white citizens, are yet declared to be criminals, liable to imprisonment, if they ride in a public coach occupied by citizens of the white race. It is scarcely just to say that a colored citizen should not object to occupying a public coach assigned to his own race. He does not object, nor, perhaps, would he object to separate coaches for his race if his rights under the law were recognized. But he objecting, and ought never to cease objecting, to the proposition that citizens of the white and black race can be adjudged criminals because they sit, or claim the right to sit, in the same public coach on a public highway.

The arbitrary separation of citizens on the basis of race while they are on a public highway is a badge of servitude wholly inconsistent with the civil freedom and the equality before the law established by the Constitution. It cannot be justified upon any legal grounds.

If evils will result from the commingling of the two races upon public highways established for the benefit of all, they will be infinitely less than those that will surely come from state legislation regulating the enjoyment of civil rights upon the basis of race. We boast of the freedom enjoyed by our people above all other peoples. But it is difficult to reconcile that boast with a state of the law which, practically, puts the brand of servitude and degradation upon a large class of our fellow citizens, our equals before the law. The thin disguise of "equal" accommodations for passengers in railroad coaches will not mislead anyone, nor atone for the wrong this day done.

The result of the whole matter is that, while this court has frequently adjudged, and at the present term has recognized the doctrine, that a State cannot, consistently with the Constitution of the United States, prevent white and black citizens, having the required qualifications for jury service, from sitting in the same jury box, it is now solemnly held that a State may prohibit white and black citizens from sitting in the same passenger coach on a public highway, or may require that they be separated by a "partition," when in the same passenger coach. May it not now be reasonably expected that astute men of the dominant race, who affect to be disturbed at the possibility that the integrity of the white race may be corrupted, or that its supremacy will be imperiled, by contact on public highways with black people, will endeavor to procure statutes requiring white and black jurors to be separated in the jury box by a "partition," and that, upon retiring from the courtroom to consult as to their verdict, such partition, if it be a moveable one, shall be taken to their consultation room and set up in such way as to prevent black jurors from coming too close to their brother jurors of the white race. If the "partition" used in the courtroom happens to be stationary, provision could be made for screens with openings through which jurors of the two races could confer as to their verdict without coming into personal contact with each other. I cannot see but that, according to the principles this day announced, such state legislation, although conceived in hostility to, and enacted for the purpose of humiliating, citizens of the United States of a particular race, would be held to be consistent with the Constitution.

I do not deem it necessary to review the decisions of state courts to which reference was made in argument. Some, and the most important, of them are wholly inapplicable because rendered prior to the adoption of the last amendments of the Constitution, when colored people had very few rights which the dominant race felt obliged to respect. Others were made at a time when public opinion in many localities was dominated by the institution of slavery, when it would not have been safe to do justice to the black man, and when, so far as the rights of blacks were concerned, race prejudice was, practically, the supreme law of the land. Those decisions cannot be guides in the era introduced by the recent amendments of the supreme law, which established universal civil freedom, gave citizenship to all born or naturalized in the United States and residing here, obliterated the race line from our systems of governments, National and State, and placed our free institutions upon the broad and sure foundation of the equality of all men before the law.

I am of the opinion that the statute of Louisiana is inconsistent with the personal liberty of citizens, white and black, in that State, and hostile to both the spirit and letter of the Constitution of the United States. If laws of like character should be enacted in the several States of the Union, the effect would be in the highest degree mischievous. Slavery, as an institution tolerated by law would, it is true, have disappeared from our country, but there would remain a power in the States, by sinister legislation, to interfere with the full enjoyment of the blessings of freedom to regulate civil rights, common to all citizens, upon the basis of race, and to place in a condition of legal inferiority a large body of American citizens now constituting a part of the political community called the People of the United States, for whom and by whom, through representatives, our government is administered. Such a system is inconsistent with the guarantee given by the Constitution to each State of a republican form of government, and may be stricken down by Congressional action, or by the courts in the discharge of their solemn duty to maintain the supreme law of the land, anything in the constitution or laws of any State to the contrary notwithstanding.

For the reasons stated, I am constrained to withhold my assent from the opinion and judgment of the majority.

It is worth noting Justice Harlan's dissent, in which he said:

[I]n view of the constitution, in the eye of the law, there is in this country no superior, dominant, ruling class of citizens. There is no caste here. Our constitution is color-blind, and neither knows nor tolerates classes among citizens. In respect of civil rights, all citizens are equal before the law. The humblest is the peer of the most powerful. The law regards man as man, and takes no account of his surroundings or of his color when his civil rights as guaranteed by the supreme law of the land are involved.[17]

Nearly 60 years later, society had changed. A generation of people born in a post-slavery United States had come of age, and many of them took a new view of race. Yet Congress had not yet acted to remedy the discriminatory effects of the *Plessy* decision years earlier. Thus, the only way for society to reverse the resonating effects from the precedential decision was to go back to the judiciary.

The *Brown v. Board of Education* case that follows was decided in 1954. The case involved a group of schoolchildren in Kansas who were forced to attend a school for black children in a segregated society. The schools were relatively equal in terms of objective factors, such as materials and resources. But they were also in stark contrast of one another, reflecting the divisive nature of segregation and its profound effects on everyday life.

The *Brown* case was brought as a class action lawsuit against the Topeka Board of Education. The schoolchildren were represented by the National Association for the Advancement of Colored People (NAACP), and it was seen at the time as one of the most important cases in the history of civil rights. Brown lost in the lower federal courts not because the courts failed to recognize the changes in society, but because its hands were tied by the precedent set in *Plessy* and only the U.S. Supreme Court could change that. Aware of this, the NAACP made a careful argument to circumvent the "separate but equal" justification for segregation set in *Plessy*. The opinion is below.

Brown v. Board of Education of Topeka[18]

MR. CHIEF JUSTICE WARREN delivered the opinion of the Court.

These cases come to us from the States of Kansas, South Carolina, Virginia, and Delaware. They are premised on different facts and different local conditions, but a common legal question justifies their consideration together in this consolidated opinion.

In each of the cases, minors of the Negro race, through their legal representatives, seek the aid of the courts in obtaining admission to the public schools of their community on a non-segregated basis. In each instance, they had been denied admission to schools attended by white children under laws requiring or permitting segregation according to race. This segregation was alleged to deprive the plaintiffs of the equal protection of the laws under the Fourteenth Amendment. In each of the cases other than the Delaware case, a three-judge federal district court denied relief to the plaintiffs on the so-called "separate but equal" doctrine announced by this Court in Plessy v. Ferguson, *163 U.S. 537. Under that doctrine, equality of treatment is accorded when the races are provided substantially equal facilities, even though these facilities be separate. In the Delaware case, the Supreme Court of Delaware adhered to that doctrine, but ordered that the plaintiffs be admitted to the white schools because of their superiority to the Negro schools.*

The plaintiffs contend that segregated public schools are not "equal" and cannot be made "equal," and that hence they are deprived of the equal protection of the laws. Because of the obvious importance of the question presented, the Court took jurisdiction. Argument was heard in the 1952 Term, and reargument was heard this Term on certain questions propounded by the Court.

Reargument was largely devoted to the circumstances surrounding the adoption of the Fourteenth Amendment in 1868. It covered exhaustively consideration of the Amendment in Congress, ratification by the states, then-existing practices in racial segregation, and the views of proponents and opponents of the Amendment. This discussion and our own investigation convince us that, although these sources cast some light, it is not enough to resolve the problem with which we are faced. At best, they are inconclusive. The most avid proponents of the post-War Amendments undoubtedly intended them to remove all legal distinctions among "all persons born or naturalized in the United States." Their opponents, just as certainly, were antagonistic to both the letter and the spirit of the Amendments and wished them to have the most limited effect. What others in

Congress and the state legislatures had in mind cannot be determined with any degree of certainty.

An additional reason for the inconclusive nature of the Amendment's history with respect to segregated schools is the status of public education at that time. In the South, the movement toward free common schools, supported by general taxation, had not yet taken hold. Education of white children was largely in the hands of private groups. Education of Negroes was almost nonexistent, and practically all of the race were illiterate. In fact, any education of Negroes was forbidden by law in some states. Today, in contrast, many Negroes have achieved outstanding success in the arts and sciences, as well as in the business and professional world. It is true that public school education at the time of the Amendment had advanced further in the North, but the effect of the Amendment on Northern States was generally ignored in the congressional debates. Even in the North, the conditions of public education did not approximate those existing today. The curriculum was usually rudimentary; ungraded schools were common in rural areas; the school term was but three months a year in many states, and compulsory school attendance was virtually unknown. As a consequence, it is not surprising that there should be so little in the history of the Fourteenth Amendment relating to its intended effect on public education.

In the first cases in this Court construing the Fourteenth Amendment, decided shortly after its adoption, the Court interpreted it as proscribing all state-imposed discriminations against the Negro race. The doctrine of "separate but equal" did not make its appearance in this Court until 1896 in the case of Plessy v. Ferguson, *supra, involving not education but transportation. American courts have since labored with the doctrine for over half a century. In this Court, there have been six cases involving the "separate but equal" doctrine in the field of public education. In* Cumming v. County Board of Education, *175 U.S. 528, and* Gong Lum v. Rice, *275 U.S. 78, the validity of the doctrine itself was not challenged. In more recent cases, all on the graduate school level, inequality was found in that specific benefits enjoyed by white students were denied to Negro students of the same educational qualifications.* Missouri ex rel. Gaines v. Canada, *305 U.S. 337;* Sipuel v. Oklahoma, *332 U.S. 631;* Sweatt v. Painter, *339 U.S. 629;* McLaurin v. Oklahoma State Regents, *339 U.S. 637. In none of these cases was it necessary to reexamine the doctrine to grant relief to the Negro plaintiff. And in* Sweatt v. Painter, *supra, the Court expressly reserved decision on the question whether* Plessy v. Ferguson *should be held inapplicable to public education.*

In the instant cases, that question is directly presented. Here, unlike Sweatt v. Painter, *there are findings below that the Negro and white schools involved have been equalized, or are being equalized, with respect to buildings, curricula, qualifications and salaries of teachers, and other "tangible" factors. Our decision, therefore, cannot turn on merely a comparison of these tangible factors in the Negro and white schools involved in each of the cases. We must look instead to the effect of segregation itself on public education.*

In approaching this problem, we cannot turn the clock back to 1868, when the Amendment was adopted, or even to 1896, when Plessy v. Ferguson *was written. We must consider public education in the light of its full development and its present place in American life throughout the Nation. Only in this way can it be determined if segregation in public schools deprives these plaintiffs of the equal protection of the laws.*

Today, education is perhaps the most important function of state and local governments. Compulsory school attendance laws and the great expenditures for education both demonstrate our recognition of the importance of education to our democratic society. It is required in the performance of our most basic public responsibilities, even service in the armed forces. It is the very foundation of good citizenship. Today it is a principal instrument in awakening the child to cultural values, in preparing him for later professional training, and in helping him to adjust normally to his environment. In these days, it is doubtful that any child may reasonably be expected to succeed in life if he is denied the opportunity of an education. Such an opportunity, where the state has undertaken to provide it, is a right which must be made available to all on equal terms.

We come then to the question presented: does segregation of children in public schools solely on the basis of race, even though the physical facilities and other "tangible" factors may be equal, deprive the children of the minority group of equal educational opportunities? We believe that it does.

In Sweatt v. Painter, *supra, in finding that a segregated law school for Negroes could not provide them equal educational opportunities, this Court relied in large part on "those qualities which are incapable of objective measurement but which make for greatness in a law school." In* McLaurin v. Oklahoma State Regents, *supra, the Court, in requiring that a Negro admitted to a white graduate school be treated like all other students, again resorted to intangible considerations: ". . . his ability to study, to engage in discussions and exchange views with other students, and, in general, to learn his profession."*

Such considerations apply with added force to children in grade and high schools. To separate them from others of similar age and qualifications solely because of their race generates a feeling of inferiority as to their status in the community that may affect their hearts and minds in a way unlikely ever to be undone. The effect of this separation on their educational opportunities was well stated by a finding in the Kansas case by a court which nevertheless felt compelled to rule against the Negro plaintiffs:

> *Segregation of white and colored children in public schools has a detrimental effect upon the colored children. The impact is greater when it has the sanction of the law, for the policy of separating the races is usually interpreted as denoting the inferiority of the negro group. A sense of inferiority affects the motivation of a child to learn. Segregation with the sanction of law, therefore, has a tendency to [retard] the educational and mental development of negro children and to deprive them of some of the benefits they would receive in a racial[ly] integrated school system.*

Whatever may have been the extent of psychological knowledge at the time of Plessy v. Ferguson, *this finding is amply supported by modern authority. Any language in* Plessy v. Ferguson *contrary to this finding is rejected.*

We conclude that, in the field of public education, the doctrine of "separate but equal" has no place. Separate educational facilities are inherently unequal. Therefore, we hold that the plaintiffs and others similarly situated for whom the actions have been brought are, by reason of the segregation complained of, deprived of the equal protection of the laws guaranteed by the Fourteenth Amendment. This disposition makes unnecessary any discussion whether such segregation also violates the Due Process Clause of the Fourteenth Amendment.

Because these are class actions, because of the wide applicability of this decision, and because of the great variety of local conditions, the formulation of decrees in these cases presents problems of considerable complexity. On reargument, the consideration of appropriate relief was necessarily subordinated to the primary question—the constitutionality of segregation in public education. We have now announced that such segregation is a denial of the equal protection of the laws. In order that we may have the full assistance of the parties in formulating decrees, the cases will be restored to the docket, and the parties are requested to present further argument on Questions 4 and 5 previously propounded by the Court for the reargument this Term. The Attorney General of the United States is again invited to participate. The Attorneys General of the states requiring or permitting segregation in public education will also be permitted to appear as amici curiae upon request to do so by September 15, 1954, and submission of briefs by October 1, 1954.

It is so Ordered

The *Brown* decision was unanimous and a welcome change in precedent. Following the decision, states began the process of desegregation, not just of schools, but of all public places that had for years been symbols of a racial divide. The decision breathed new life into the civil rights movement and paved the way for the Civil Rights Act of 1964.

Besides serving as a harbinger for the end of segregation, the *Brown* decision also serves a very useful purpose in explaining how the American legal mind works. Consider the argument made in *Plessy*. In an effort to challenge a law that required separate railcars for black and white passengers, lawyers for Mr. Plessy crafted a unique argument that Mr. Plessy's Fourteenth Amendment right to protect his reputation as a black man was being taken away by the courts. Consider for a moment the language of Section 1 of that Amendment:

> *All persons born or naturalized in the United States, and subject to the jurisdiction thereof, are citizens of the United States and of the state wherein they reside. No state shall make or enforce any law which shall abridge the privileges or immunities of citizens of the United States; nor shall any state deprive any person of life, liberty, or property, without due process of law; nor deny to any person within its jurisdiction the equal protection of the laws.*[19]

The Amendment was still a relatively new creation, so little precedent existed to explain how it worked in practice. The Court emphasized that while the Amendment has the clear purpose of establishing absolute equality of the races, that does not prevent states from drawing political distinctions that maintain equality despite those distinctions.

In response to the petitioner's argument, the Court explained that reputation as a black man could indeed (for purposes of this case, anyway) be seen as property. And before the state takes away that property, the owner of such property must have his due process rights respected, which often means he has a right to a hearing. However, the argument fails to capture the Court's sympathies. The reputation as a black man would be taken away if Mr. Plessy were forced by the state to sit in the car for white passengers, and likewise the reputation of a white man would be taken away if he were forced to sit in a car for black passengers.

However, since Mr. Plessy has no "right" to sit in the white passenger car, nothing was taken away from him when he was removed from that car.

Fast forward 60 years to the *Brown* decision. Note that the petitioner used a wholly new argument to reframe the issue altogether. In that case, the issue was not whether the reputation of the children was being taken away or that any property at all was being impacted. Rather, the argument went back to the meaning of the Fourteenth Amendment, which even *Plessy* recognized as an effort to create quality among the races. The attorney in *Brown* contended that by forcing black children to go to a separate school, regardless of its objective equality with the white children's school, the children were subjectively unequal. Being apart from other children from the school district created a perceived inequality and ingrained in those children a sense of inferiority that they would carry with them into adulthood. This was precisely the issue the Fourteenth Amendment was designed to remedy. And this was an argument that received the sympathetic ear of the Court, leading to the demise of *Plessy*.

Judicial Review and Federalism

We looked at the concept of judicial review earlier when we discussed the *Marbury v. Madison* decision. Remember that this central concept to our system of precedent means that the courts are the guardians of the Constitution and the gatekeepers to the law, even though laws are made by Congress and not the judiciary. To get a better sense of how powerful this concept is, let's consider a recent and controversial issue, one that impacts many non-U.S. citizen attorneys working in the United States—immigration.

The United States shares a border with Mexico, and many states along that border see immigrants crossing unlawfully into the United States. Accordingly, they have an interest in seeing the enforcement of immigration law to protect their economies and maintain security in their states. However, immigration law is one of a handful of areas of federal law that is largely out of the reach of a state's legislative powers. Nevertheless, for a variety of reasons, some states have taken it upon themselves to pass their own immigration laws.

Arizona has been the most aggressive in passing its own immigration legislation. In 2010, the Arizona state legislature enacted Senate Bill 1070, which set out to empower Arizona state police officers to check the immigration status of those whom they suspected to be unlawfully present in the United States. On its face, this section of the law appears to promote racial and national origin discrimination, given that an officer would likely only inquire of non-whites. However, Arizona claimed that it had the authority to pass such as law because it was only attempting to enforce existing federal laws.

The bill had been drafted by strong opponents of unlawful immigration, and the goal was to craft a model law that could be adopted by other states affected by such individuals.[20] And Arizona's governor stated that state police officers would be properly trained to avoid any risks of discrimination or racial profiling. However, that was not the legal challenge that the law ultimately faced.

The Obama administration filed suit before the law took effect, challenging it not on equal protection grounds, but rather because it was attempting to usurp exclusive federal power over immigration. State laws that conflict with or prevent compliance with federal laws are generally considered to be pre-empted. This is a concept that emanates from the supremacy clause of Article VI of the Constitution, which says, in relevant part:

> *This Constitution, and the laws of the United States which shall be made in pursuance thereof; and all treaties made, or which shall be made, under the authority of the United States, shall be the supreme law of the land; and the judges in every state shall be bound thereby, anything in the Constitution or laws of any State to the contrary notwithstanding.*[21]

Arizona was attempting to pass its own legislation to enforce existing federal laws on immigration. Federal power to regulate immigration resides both in the naturalization clause of Article I of the Constitution and from a variety of cases in the late 19th century that took most immigration powers away from the states. Similarly, the U.S. Congress passed several major federal statutes in the 20th century, including the Immigration and Nationality Act of 1952, which set out broad federal power over immigration. But if Arizona was only enforcing existing federal laws, how does that create a conflict with federal immigration law?

Consider the following excerpts from the U.S. Department of Justice brief on behalf of the United States:

> *In our constitutional system, the federal government has preeminent authority to regulate immigration matters . . . In administering these laws, the federal agencies balance the complex—and often competing—objectives that animate federal immigration law and policy. Although states may exercise their police power in a manner that has an incidental or indirect effect on aliens, a state may not establish its own immigration policy or enforce state laws in a manner that interferes with the federal immigration laws. The Constitution and the federal immigration laws do not permit the development of a patchwork of state and local immigration policies throughout the country.*
>
> . . .
>
> *S.B. 1070 pursues only one goal—"attrition"—and ignores the many other objectives that Congress has established for the federal immigration system. And even in pursuing attrition, S.B. 1070 disrupts federal enforcement priorities and resources that focus on aliens who pose a threat to national security or public safety. If allowed to go into effect, S.B. 1070's mandatory enforcement scheme will conflict with and undermine the federal government's careful balance of immigration enforcement priorities and objectives. For example, it will impose significant and counterproductive burdens on the federal agencies charged with enforcing the national immigration scheme, diverting resources and attention from the dangerous aliens who the federal government targets as its top enforcement*

> *priority. It will cause the detention and harassment of authorized visitors, immigrants, and citizens who do not have or carry identification documents specified by the statute, or who otherwise will be swept into the ambit of S.B. 1070's "attrition through enforcement" approach. It will conflict with longstanding federal law governing the registration, smuggling, and employment of aliens. It will altogether ignore humanitarian concerns, such as the protections available under federal law for an alien who has a well-founded fear of persecution or who has been the victim of a natural disaster. And it will interfere with vital foreign policy and national security interests by disrupting the United States' relationship with Mexico and other countries.*[22]

There is no question that the regulation of the entry and exit of non-citizens is within the purview of the U.S. Congress. Article I of the U.S. Constitution establishes the "naturalization" power within the federal government, giving Congress alone the power to decide who is worthy of citizenship:

> *To establish a uniform rule of naturalization, and uniform laws on the subject of bankruptcies throughout the United States*[23]

But how did this power over the naturalization of non-citizens turn into a power to regulate immigration law in general? To answer that question, we again turn to the courts to understand how they applied their interpretation of the law to this field.

Excerpt from Kevin J. Fandl, *Putting States Out of the Immigration Law Enforcement Business*, 9.2 Harv. L. & Pol'y Rev. (forthcoming 2015).[24]

Prior to 1891, the federal government did not have the will or the resources to take on broad immigration enforcement. Ports were largely operated by states, and immigrants entered the United States at the discretion of the local port director. At that time, immigrants largely arrived by sea from Europe or Asia, rather than across land borders. Arriving immigrants faced a hodgepodge of regulations depending on the port at which they landed. Port directors took advantage of their authority, often in a discriminatory fashion, charging intending immigrants exorbitant fees and threatening them with deportation or incarceration.[25] The inconsistent state rules affecting arriving immigrants led the U.S. Supreme Court to clarify the role of the states in regulating arriving immigrants.

Although the Supreme Court began striking down state laws on immigration as early as the mid-nineteenth century,[26] it was toward the end of that century following a proliferation of discriminatory laws toward Asian immigrants when the Court dramatically shifted the balance of immigration power from states to the federal government. They asserted this role most aggressively in the 1876 Chy Lung case, which was brought by a group of female immigrants from China who were detained by the California port director, demanding bonds of $500 each before he would allow them entry to the United States. Upon refusal to pay, some were detained by the director pending deportation. The intending immigrants challenged their detention and the authority of the port director to unilaterally determine the requirements for entry into the United States. The case made its way to the U.S. Supreme Court, which ultimately struck down the California statute allowing their state port director discretion over immigration.

In the Chy Lung case, the Court said, "It is hardly possible to conceive a statute more skilfully [sic] framed, to place in the hands of a single man the power to prevent entirely vessels engaged in a foreign trade, say with China, from carrying passengers, or to compel them to submit to systematic extortion of the grossest kind."[27] The Court then criticized states for not taking into account the effects of their immigration laws on the international obligations of the United States. "[I]f citizens of our own government were treated by any foreign nation as subjects of the Emperor of China have been actually treated under this law, no administration could withstand the call for a demand on such government for redress."[28]

Finally, seeing this as an opportunity to clarify the role of states and the federal government in the enforcement of immigration law:

> *The passage of laws which concern the admission of citizens and subjects of foreign nations to our shores belongs to Congress, and not to the States. It has the power to regulate commerce with foreign nations: the responsibility for the character of those regulations, and for the manner of their execution, belongs solely to the national government. If it be otherwise, a single State can, at her pleasure, embroil us in disastrous quarrels with other nations.*[29]

Rather than looking to the naturalization clause of the U.S. Constitution, the court here explained that immigration is a matter of foreign commerce, which is exclusively a federal power according to Article I § 8. And while the naturalization clause (immediately following the commerce clause) leaves no doubt that a state is expressly precluded from promulgating statutes that affect in any way the requirements for citizenship and the naturalization process, it is the commerce clause that situates broad immigration enforcement powers in the hands of the federal government.

Shortly after the Chy Lung case, the Court gave Congress the expansive immigration enforcement power that they previously lacked. In *Fong Yue Ting v. United States,* the Court concluded that the federal government had the "absolute and unqualified" power to deport aliens in the interest of national sovereignty. These combined decisions established what is referred to today as "pure" immigration authority—the power of the federal government to control the entry, naturalization, and deportation of non-citizens, as well as most immigration law enforcement powers.

Later cases, such as *United States v. Curtiss-Wright Export Corp.*, strengthened the argument that matters of foreign affairs are within the exclusive purview of the federal government. Only the federal government can speak as the representative of the

United States in front of other nations. Thus, if immigration is a matter of foreign relations, there can be little doubt that only the federal government is empowered to regulate the field of pure immigration issues.

However, pure immigration issues were not the only immigration issues. States maintained that neither the commerce nor the naturalization clause prevented them from promulgating laws regulating the acts of immigrants within their state borders. And they were right—to a degree. The Court in *DeCanas v. Bica* upheld a California statute that made it unlawful for an employer to knowingly employ a non-citizen not entitled to lawful residence if they can show that such employment would have an adverse effect on lawful workers. In the decision, Justice Blackmun said, "the Court has never held that every state enactment which in any way deals with aliens is a regulation of immigration and thus per se preempted by this constitutional immigration power, whether latent or exercised."

The DeCanas case has been interpreted to mean that state legislatures are allowed to regulate immigration so long as they do so in an area that is not expressly controlled by the federal government. For instance, the Court later upheld state statutes that restricted the issuance of driver's licenses to unlawful migrants,[30] or set forth special probate rules for non-citizens.[31] Accordingly, if the federal government has not legislated specifically in these areas of immigration law, and so long as the state statutes do not conflict with other federal laws, states may be permitted to legislate here. However, this has become an increasingly narrow grant of power.

Advocates for more restrictive immigration laws have consistently argued that the states have the ability to pass laws that would place immigration law enforcement authority squarely within the hands of state authorities.[32] Pro-immigrant rights groups have favored the argument that the federal government is the only entity with the legal authority to touch immigrants.[33] This is not a question of whether the federal government can exclusively control immigration law, but rather whether they have done so. Given that the Constitution does not definitively answer this question, states have attempted to fill the void with their own legislation, leaving it up to the courts and congress to clarify the scope of federal immigration power on a case-by-case basis.

. . .

Arizona's SB 1070 was intended to serve as a model law that other states could adopt to take more aggressive control over their immigration law enforcement practices. The law attempted to set forth a model for "concurrent enforcement" of state and federal law affecting immigrants.[34] To achieve this goal, it focused on four powers for state and local law enforcement: 1) ability to arrest immigrants for failure to carry proper immigration documentation; 2) ability to arrest immigrants without a warrant; 3) ability to arrest for attempts to secure unlawful employment; and 4) mandate to inquire about immigration status during lawful stops.

Failure to carry proper immigrant documentation or applying for unlawful employment were already federal misdemeanors. Arizona's law made them state misdemeanors as well. By adopting equivalent legislation in state law, Arizona sought the ability to enforce the spirit of the federal law without waiting for federal officials to take action. But their self-designation as federal sidekicks was short-lived.

The Arizona decision is important for our understanding not only of the relationship between lawmaking powers of the federal and state governments, but also in how both the legislatures and courts apply their legal interpretations of precedent in a manner that benefits them most. Arizona here capitalized on the Supreme Court's language that seemed to permit states to pass immigration regulations so long as those regulations did not conflict with those already enacted by the federal government. This was interpreted by the federal government to mean that a state could regulate things like business licenses issued to immigrants or the issuance of driver's licenses to immigrants, because the federal government had not issued any regulations on those topics. Arizona went one step further and argued that it is not only situations in which the federal government has not *enacted* regulations where the states can act; it is also where the federal government is not enforcing those regulations.

Arizona's novel approach was premised on the concept of "concurrent legislation," meaning that the state passed the same laws and enacted the same regulations that exist in federal law; however, the Arizona laws empowered their own law enforcement authorities to enforce those laws within their state. The court didn't object to the use of concurrent legislation *per se*, but it concluded that applying different enforcement practices in the same area of law amounted to a usurpation of federal power by the state.

> *The U.S. Supreme Court, in a 5–3 decision, ruled in June 2012 that the "concurrent" laws were preempted by federal law. Relying on both the naturalization clause and foreign relations as the bases for broad federal power over immigration, Justice Kennedy affirmed that it is up to federal immigration authorities to determine if and when to enforce federal immigration laws. Giving states equivalent powers would take away that federal discretion and negatively impact federal policy regarding non-citizens. As a model law, Arizona's SB1070 fell far short of what the federal courts were willing to allow.*[35]

It is worth noting here that numerous states, including Alabama, Utah, and South Carolina, passed laws modeled on Arizona's Senate Bill 1070 and many of them are being challenged by the federal government.

Notes

1 *Marbury v. Madison*, 5 U.S. 137, 158 (1803) at 167–168.

2 The Act gave the Supreme Court the power "to issue writs of mandamus, in cases warranted by the principles and usages of law, to any courts appointed, or persons holding office, under the authority of the United States." (*Marbury* at 173).

3 *Marbury* at 174 (emphasis added).
4 *Marbury* at 177–178.
5 Thomas Jefferson, Letter to William Jarvis (September 28, 1820) in *The Writings of Thomas Jefferson*, published collection of letters, https://archive.org/stream/writingsofthomas10jeffiala/writingsofthomas10jeffiala_djvu.txt.
6 *Marbury* at 178.
7 http://worldjusticeproject.org/blog/constitution-india-holy-cow.
8 http://www.annistonstar.com/article_c928bd51-fbf1–5056-a30c-1bf4b19eb012.html?mode=jqm.
9 Consider Colombia, for instance, which includes 380 Articles in its 1991 constitution.
10 U.S. Const. Amend. II.
11 *United States v. Miller*, 307 U.S. 174 (1939).
12 554 U.S. 570 (2008).
13 Firearms Control Regulations Act of 1975.
14 U.S. Const. Amend. XIII.
15 U.S. Const. Amend. XIV.
16 163 U.S. 537 (1896).
17 *Plessy*, 163 U.S., at 559.
18 347 U.S. 483 (1954).
19 U.S. Const. Amend. XIV, § 1.
20 Alabama, Utah, and South Carolina passed similar bills shortly thereafter.
21 U.S. Const. Art. VI.
22 Complaint filed by Assistant Attorney General Tony West (July 6, 2010).
23 U.S. Cont. Art. I § 8.
24 Kevin J. Fandl, *Putting States Out of the Immigration Law Enforcement Business*, 9.2 Harv. L. & Pol'y Rev. (forthcoming 2015).
25 For example, Asian immigrants arriving on the west coast were often subjected to high fees and threats of deportation at a time when such immigrants were largely disfavored.
26 See, e.g., Jennifer Chacon, *Who is Responsible for U.S. Immigration Policy?*, 14 ABA Insights on Law and Society 3 (2014).
27 *Chy Lung v. Freeman*, 92 U.S. 275, 279 (1876).
28 Id.
29 Id. at 280.
30 *John Doe No. 1 v. Georgia Dep't of Pub. Safety*, 147 F. Supp. 2d 1369 (N.D.Ga.2001).
31 *Clark v. Allen*, 331 U.S. 503 (1947).
32 See, e.g., Kris Kobach, *State and Local Authority to Enforce Immigration Law: A Unified Approach to Stopping Terrorists*, Center for Immigration Studies Backgrounder (June 2004), http://www.cis.org/StateEnforcement-LocalEnforcement.
33 See, e.g., National Immigration Law Center (March 2011), http://www.nilc.org/oppose-state-imm-regulation-2011–03.html.
34 See, e.g., John Schwartz, *A Law Facing a Though Road Through the Courts*, NY Times (April 28, 2010).
35 Kevin J. Fandl, *Putting States Out of the Immigration Law Enforcement Business*, 9.2 Harv. L. & Pol'y Rev. (forthcoming 2015).

4

THE SEDUCTION OF DEDUCTION

Logic

> The study of logic is a lost art.[1]

Crafting a legal argument is no easy task. But in common law jurisdictions, it may be even more difficult than in the rest of the world. Legal reasoning in the common law relies on logic, principally through the use of the syllogism. In this section, we will examine the syllogism and how it can be used to formulate legal arguments that are rooted in multiple cases.

Deductive logic refers to the application of a general legal principle, such as a statute or regulation, to reach a specific conclusion in a single case. The following is an example of legal reasoning through deduction:

> Failure of the Seller to deliver conforming goods allows the Buyer to reject those goods.
> Jones failed to deliver conforming goods to Smith.
> Therefore, Smith may reject those goods.

This approach is frequently applied when a clear rule of law exists and there is little doubt about its applicability to the case. In these cases, the lawyer's role is to debate interpretation of the law as applied to the facts rather than the existence of the rule itself. In the hypothetical example above, this might mean that Jones's lawyer will argue over the meaning of "conforming goods," but it is unlikely he would argue that the rule stated in the first premise is wrong.

Let's look at an example in the caselaw:

- Unequal educational facilities are not permitted under the Constitution.
- A separate educational facility for black children is inherently unequal.
- Therefore a separate educational facility for black children is not permitted under the Constitution.[2]

These premises are derived from the *Brown v. Board of Education* case, which we discussed in Chapter 3. The first premise, known as the major premise, states the rule that is extracted from the Constitution, a statute, a case, or another primary legal source. The second premise, known as the minor premise, identifies the fact from the particular case. And the final premise, or the conclusion, is the application of the general principle of law (major premise) to the specific factual situation (minor premise). If the first two premises are true, the conclusion must be true. All that remains to be argued is whether the first two premises are in fact true.

The deductive logic approach is likely the most comfortable for lawyers from civil law countries, where extensive legal rules guide the arguments made by attorneys.

> *Law, considered as a science, consists of certain principles or doctrines. To have such a mastery of these as to be able to apply them with constant facility and certainty to the ever-tangled skein of human affairs, is what constitutes a true lawyer; and hence to acquire that mastery should be the business of every earnest student of law. Each of these doctrines has arrived at its present state by slow degrees; in other words, it is a growth, extending in many cases through centuries. This growth is to be traced in the main through a series of cases, and much the shortest and best, if not the only way of mastering the doctrine effectively is by studying the cases in which it is embodied.*[3]
>
> *[L]egal reasoning entails a practice of argumentation. The reasons given for the conclusions reached are to be measured by their persuasiveness, not by reference to some established true state of affairs.*[4]

The Syllogism

The heart of U.S. legal reasoning is found in the logical device known as the syllogism. Fundamentally, the syllogism draws a conclusion by applying a general idea to a specific circumstance. Once the general idea has been clearly identified, it is only a matter of applying that idea to the circumstances of a particular case in order to yield the same outcome that the general rule suggests. The logical approach is as follows:

> Major Premise (Rule) + Minor Premise (Application of Rule) = Conclusion

Or, in logical statements, we might state:

> The Fourth Amendment prohibits a police search without a warrant or probable cause. (Major Premise)
> The police officer searched the defendant's car without a warrant or probable cause. (Minor Premise)
> Therefore, the police officer violated the Fourth Amendment. (Conclusion)

We can represent this inductive syllogistic analysis graphically as follows:

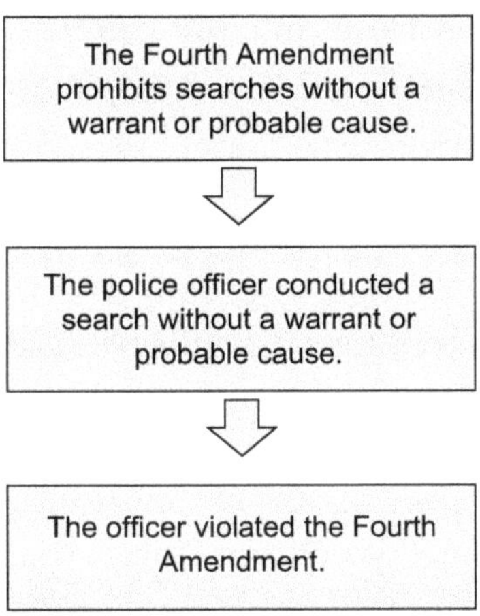

Figure 4.1

Inductive reasoning and the use of the syllogism to discern the likely outcome from the application of a single rule to a single case is a clear and efficient way to manage cases. In a civil law system in which many black letter[5] rules exist to guide attorneys in crafting their arguments, the inductive reasoning process is relatively straightforward. What remains to be debated is the interpretation of the facts, but not necessarily the application of the law once the facts have been established. Unfortunately, this is not often the case in common law jurisdictions.

Reliance on a codified rule or a clear guiding principle from caselaw is often ill-placed in common law legal analysis. There is rarely one single source to which attorneys can turn to guide their analyses. "Unlike science, the law has multiple sources. In hard cases, the law is fundamentally indeterminate. And unlike science, the law is volitional, not phenomenological. The root premises of law are value judgments. Though law is logical and rational in form, in substance it is evaluative, the result of intentional value choices."[6]

In my lectures to civil law students, I am always met with shocked faces when I explain that a case brief for a single issue may contain 10, 20, or more cases as guiding precedent. Attorneys in the United States are well-versed in the nature of legal argument and understand that rules need to be made, not found. This means extracting elements of rules from many cases and piecing them together to ultimately formulate the rule that will apply to your case. This is no small task, but this is critical in understanding the American legal mind.

Deductive Reasoning

We just learned the value of applying a single rule to a case in order to convince the court that a general principle should guide its decision in a specific case. But as I mentioned above, an American lawyer will typically want to craft his or her own rule rather than applying a single rule from a case or statute, if one even exists. The advantage of having your own rule is that you understand the nuances of that rule because it was crafted from carefully analyzed elements as discussed in important cases. This attorney has the advantage of knowing the nature of the rule's creation, its evolution through precedential history, and the debates about the elements that may be necessary to fit the rule around his client's facts.

Deductive reasoning is the reverse of the inductive reasoning process. To deduce a general rule, deductive reasoning requires examination of several specific instances. In other words, a rule must be created by extracting critical elements from multiple cases. "A legal argument that is a cable is one that weaves together the different kinds of legal argument. A brief or judicial opinion that cites text, intent, precedent, tradition, and policy, all tending toward a single interpretation of the law, is far more persuasive than one that utilizes a single modality. When every method of argument points to the same result, it creates an impression of inevitability."[7]

Before getting into the structure of a deductive argument, it is important to note that crafting a rule through deductive reasoning is more of an art than a science. Because you are weaving together a series of certain outcomes from cases to make a rule that does not exist yet in a case, your result is uncertain. Your "rule" is based upon the precedents that you selected, and it is likely that your counterpart on the other side of the courtroom has gone to lengths to discredit your sources and to select their own. Ultimately, it will be up to the judge to decide which rule should apply to the case.

Let's examine the logical structure of a deductive argument:

> Rule from Case A + Rule from Case B + Rule from case C. . .= General Rule

Or, applying this to a logical case:

> In Case A, the court upheld a finding of material breach where the breaching party delivered goods ten days after the delivery deadline.

In Case B, the court upheld a finding of material breach where the breaching party notified the non-breaching party of delay and did not deliver the goods until 30 days later.

In Case C, the court denied a claim of material breach where the breaching party delivered the goods five days after the delivery deadline.

General Rule: Goods delivered without notice of delay at least ten days after the delivery deadline constitute material breach; goods delivered with or without notification at least 30 days past the delivery deadline constitute material breach.

This general rule would be crafted on many cases, each of which will help the drafter to draw the contours of that rule. The established rule here does not exist in any case or statute, so the attorney will need to explain the bases for this rule by describing the relevant cases from which it came. The entire case upon which a certain element is based (e.g., Case A above) does not need to be described in detail—only enough detail to understand that court's reasoning for setting forth that finding is required.

How many cases do you need to craft an effective rule? There is no winning number in the literature, but clearly the more cases you use, the more likely you are to be successful in convincing the judge that your rule should be observed. One case found that a rule based upon five specific instances was inappropriate:

> *Based on the five patients [Dr. Scheribel] has observed with cataracts induced by radiation therapy, he developed his "binding universal rule" that he applied to O'Conner, thus committing the logical fallacy known as Converse Accident (hasty generalization). . . . It occurs when a person erroneously creates a general rule from observing too few cases. Dr. Scheribel has illogically created a "binding universal rule" based upon insufficient data. For example, observing the value of opiates when administered by a physician to alleviate the pains of those who are seriously ill, one may be led to propose*

that narcotics be made available to everyone. Or considering the effect of alcohol only on those who indulge in it to excess, one may conclude that all liquor is harmful and urge that its sale and use should be forbidden by law. Such reasoning is erroneous.[8]

Examining this in graphical form, we might perceive the following deductive logic diagram:

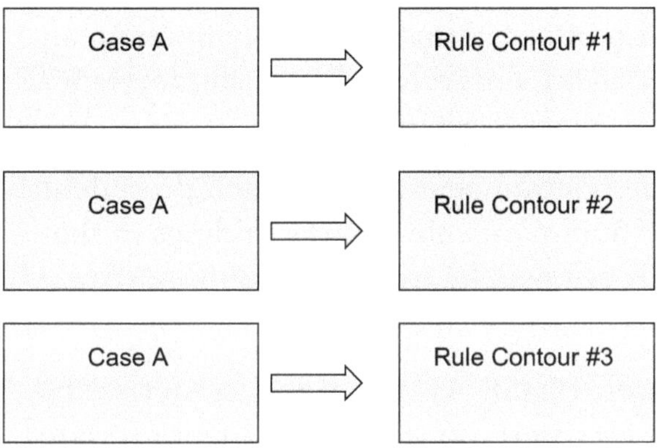

Figure 4.2

Applying inductive reasoning to create a rule means that you will have to read all of the relevant cases that address facts similar to those of your client. You will need these in order to prepare your argument for your brief to the court. Legal research is beyond the scope of this book,[9] so we will begin with the assumption that you have gathered both primary and secondary authorities that have similar fact patterns as those faced by your client. Once you have those authorities, the process that you will follow looks like this:

Step 1: Break your client's legal issue down into factual elements. You will use these elements as sections of your argument later.

Example: Your client is a Japanese car manufacturer and entered into a contract with a distributor in

Puerto Rico to sell its cars there. The contract contained a binding arbitration clause. Poor sales have led to a dispute and one of the claims involves antitrust (anti-competition) law. Your client went to court to compel arbitration, but the defendant successfully argued that statutory antitrust claims are too complex to go to arbitration. You are appealing that finding.[10]

Elements: Is an international contract containing an arbitration clause enforceable? Is a statutory antitrust claim subject to arbitration?

Step 2: Identify the relevant analysis from each precedent that you found. Summarize the court's findings in that section as briefly as possible, usually in no more than a few sentences.

Defendant's cases: [CASE A] "the rights conferred by the antitrust laws were of a character inappropriate for enforcement by arbitration."[11]

[CASE B] Nothing prevents a party from excluding statutory claims, including antitrust actions, from a contract's arbitration clause.[12]

Your Client's cases: [CASE 1] In international cases, if the parties agree to arbitrate certain issues, courts must respect their decision to do so.[13]

[CASE 2] "The liberal federal policy favoring arbitration agreements, manifested by this provision and the Act as a whole, is at bottom a policy guaranteeing the enforcement of private contractual arrangements: the Act simply creates a body of federal substantive law establishing and regulating the duty to honor an agreement to arbitrate."[14]

[CASE 3] Courts are required to "rigorously enforce agreements to arbitrate."[15]

Step 3: Determine how this analysis affects your client's situation and organize the cases into the elements of your client's case.

Element: Is an international contract containing an arbitration clause enforceable?

Application: Courts are required to enforce contractual agreements to arbitrate [CASE 3]. Unless there is an indication of fraud, courts liberally interpret mutually agreed upon agreements to arbitrate [CASE 2].

Element: Is a statutory antitrust claim subject to arbitration?

Application: Though parties are free to exclude statutory claims from arbitration [CASE B], courts are required to enforce the agreements entered into by the parties [CASE 2, 3]. In international agreements in particular, even complex statutory issues such as antitrust disputes, which some domestic cases have excluded from the scope of arbitrability [CASE B], are enforced when the contract is international in nature [CASE 1].

Step 4: Craft your rule based upon the elements that you have discussed. This rule will be the guiding principle for the remainder of your argument.

RULE: In international contracts, courts must enforce mutually agreed upon arbitration clauses even if they include complex statutory claims.

Though it seems odd to craft the rule *after* the application of cases, working in this order helps you to organize the essential elements of the rule that you will need to craft a clear and precise rule. Working in reverse, you will find that you are piecing together elements of the rule with each new case, potentially changing the direction of your argument. Your goal should be to let the rule *fall out* of your analysis rather than to use an incomplete rule to guide your analysis.

Now, let's put all of this together. Using the same case referenced above, here is what this process looks like:

ISSUE: Is an arbitration clause in an international contract binding on statutory antitrust claims where the parties so agreed?

Figure 4.3

No clear rule exists in a statute or caselaw. Apply inductive reasoning.

Case 1: Significant deference to party's arbitration agreements in international contracts.

Case 2: Courts favor arbitration agreements when mutually agreed upon by the parties.

Case 3: Courts rigorously enforce arbitration agreements in contracts.

RULE: In international contracts, courts must enforce mutually agreed upon arbitration clauses even if they include complex statutory claims.

Figure 4.4

Now that we have a rule, apply deductive reasoning to your client's case.

APPLICATION: Our client should be able to enforce the arbitration agreement on the antitrust claim because this is an international contract and the parties mutually agreed to arbitrate such claims.

Figure 4.5

From a non-common law perspective, it may seem a bit unusual to be crafting your own rules to support your arguments. But bear in mind that both parties to the transaction or litigation will engage in this process, often using different interpretations of the very same cases. Ultimately, it will be up to the judge to weigh the legal arguments and determine the soundness of the proposed rules.

Notes

1 Benjamin Jowett (trans.), *The Dialogues of Plato: Translated into English, with Analyses and Introductions*, vol 1. , 279–301 (1901).
2 Ruggero J. Aldisert, et al., *Logic for Law Students: How to Think Like a Lawyer*, 69 U. Pitt. L. Rev. 1 (2007).
3 Christopher Langdell, *A Selection of Cases on the Law of Contracts* vi (1871).
4 Donald H.J. Hermann, *Legal Reasoning as Argumentation*, 12 N. Ky. L. Rev. 467, 507 (1985). See also Linda Levine and Kurt Saunders, *Thinking Like a Rhetor*, 43 J. Legal Educ. 108 (1993).
5 "Black letter" law refers to written statutes and codes.
6 Wilson Huhn, *The Use and Limits of Deductive Logic in Legal Reasoning*, 42 Santa Clara L. Rev. 813 (2002) at 22.
7 Id. at 36.
8 Aldisert, supra note 2, at 113–114 (internal quotations and citations omitted).
9 For more information about effective legal research, consider reviewing Kevin Fandl, *Narrowing the Gap: Legal English for the New International Legal Practitioner* (2013).
10 Based upon Mitsubishi Motors Corp. v. Soler Chrysler-Plymouth, 473 U.S. 614 (1985).
11 *Mitsubishi* at 621, citing American Safety Equipment Corp. v. J.P. Maguire & Co., 391 F.2d 821 (CA2 1968) (internal quotation omitted).
12 *Prima Paint Corp. v. Flood & Conkilin Mfg.*, 388 U.S. 395, 406 (1967).
13 *Mitsubishi* at 621, citing Scherk v. Alberto-Culver Co., 417 U.S. 506, 515–520 (1974).
14 *Mitsubishi* at 625, citing Moses H. Cone Memorial Hospital v. Mercury Construction Corp., 460 U.S. 1, 24 (1983).
15 *Dean Witter Reynolds Inc. v. Byrd*, 470 U.S. 213, 221 (1985).

5

ARGUING BY ANALOGY

The Creative Lawyer

In the previous chapter, we examined the most common forms of legal analysis—inductive and deductive reasoning. But there is another form of argument that is applied when crafting a rule is impossible. This is known as argument by analogy.

"Edward Levi, the foremost American authority on the role of analogy in the law, described analogical reasoning as a three step process: 1) establish similarities between two cases, 2) announce the rule of law embedded in the first case, and 3) apply the rule of law to the second case . . . Analogy, in contrast, makes one-to-one comparisons that require no generalizations or reliance on universal rules. In the language of logicians, analogy is a process of reasoning from the particular to the particular."[1]

Consider the following case:

A passenger on a steamboat occupies a stateroom on that boat. While on the boat, the passenger is robbed by an intruder that broke into his room. The passenger sues the steamboat operator and the question to the court is about the level of care (duty) the steamboat operator owes a passenger in a stateroom. No cases address this very issue, so deductive and inductive reasoning cannot be applied.

The parties provide analogies to support their position. The plaintiff (passenger) argues that a stateroom on a steamboat is equivalent to a room at an Inn (hotel). The defendant (steamboat operator) argues that a stateroom on a steamboat is more like an open sleeping chamber on a passenger train (not a sleeping compartment but rather an open room where several passengers can sleep).

The court concluded that the analogy between the Inn and the stateroom on a steamboat was more appropriate and, thus, the steamboat operator had the higher duty of care that an Innkeeper has to his guests than a train conductor would have to those in a sleeping chamber.[2]

Arguing by analogy requires the lawyer to put on their creative hat and to find scenarios in cases that would be analogous to the outcome that the lawyer wants for his client. This is used most often in cases where no statute or precedent clearly addresses the issue. These are often called "cases of first impression" or "novel" cases. Novel cases arise frequently and courts are often faced with the need to create new precedent where none previously existed. This trailblazing approach is driven by the arguments of the lawyers, who each assert their own opinions about what the law should be. Let's examine a recent case to see how argument by analogy can be weaved into a case of international contracts.

Cross-Cultural Arguments in the U.S. Judicial System: The Case of BG Group and Argentina

The best way to see the American legal mind in action is to watch the drama unfold in the courtroom. Listening to oral arguments, especially in an appellate case, will be the best avenue to experience the way that American lawyers employ analogies and deductive logic to a narrow set of facts. Given that these oral arguments cannot be captured on the pages of a book, the next best thing is to look at the briefs filed in advance of oral argument by the representatives of both parties. The logic is the same, though the passion is certainly removed.

A recent U.S. Supreme Court case dealing with British investments in Argentina may be the best example of a cross-border and cross-cultural legal argument played out in American courts. The case, *BG Group v. Republic of Argentina*, dealt with a rather simple issue, captured concisely in the plaintiff's brief to the Court:

In disputes involving a multi-staged dispute resolution process, does a court or instead the arbitrator determine whether a precondition to arbitration has been satisfied?[3]

The first thing you may notice from this issue statement is that it is truly concise. This is, of course, intentional. An issue of law that arises on appeal from a trial court will often include an array of elements and complaints, including arguments about jurisdiction, justiciability, precedent, and so forth. As a party works through the appeals process, the legal issue is whittled down to a more concise and focused question of law. By the time the issue arrives at the U.S. Supreme Court, the issue is usually a single, precisely crafted question of law, like the one above. Every word in that statement was carefully chosen to reflect not only the legal issue, but also the position of the party stating it. Compare that to the issue statement put forth by the defendant:

> *Whether a federal court with jurisdiction over an application to vacate an arbitral award may, under* First Options of Chicago v. Kaplan, *514 U.S. 938 (1995), independently decide whether there exists a valid and binding agreement to arbitrate, predicated on the terms of a bilateral investment treaty?*[4]

Note that this issue, drafted by civil law attorneys aware that they were operating in a common law court, is somewhat longer but again skewed toward the defendant. You can tell immediately that the defendant is attempting to convince the court that it has the ability to override the findings of an arbitrator. But before we get into the details about the arguments and legal reasoning, let's look more closely at the facts of this case.

Background to the BG Group Dispute

The United Kingdom entered into a bilateral investment treaty (BIT) with the Republic of Argentina in 1990. That agreement, which protected investors against state expropriation of funds, among other things, included a dispute resolution provision that investors would be able to rely upon in the event of an alleged violation of the terms of the agreement. This included the fair and equitable treatment of those investments by the state in which the investments are made:

> *Investments of investors of each Contracting Party shall at all times be accorded fair and equitable treatment and . . . [n]either Contracting Party shall in any way impair by unreasonable or discriminatory measures the management, maintenance, use, enjoyment or disposal of investments in its territory of investors of the other Contracting Party.*[5]

The treaty included, as most BITs do, a dispute settlement provision. The relevant section of that treaty authorizes a party to submit a dispute:

> *to the decision of the competent tribunal of the Contracting Party in whose territory the investment was made* [i.e., *a local court] . . . [and permits arbitration, as relevant here,] where, after a period of eighteen months has elapsed from the moment when the dispute was submitted to [that] tribunal . . . the said tribunal has not given its final decision.*[6]

BG Group, a British firm, owned a majority stake in the Argentine company MetroGas, which distributed natural gas in Buenos Aires. When the Argentine government awarded BG Group the license to distribute natural gas through MetroGas, BG Group was promised that gas tariffs would be calculated in dollars and that they would receive a reasonable investment return. This changed during the Argentinian economic crisis between 1998 and 2001, which led Argentina to take measures to protect its markets.

As part of its protective measures, Argentina amended the agreement with BG Group by converting the "dollars" provision to pesos, which significantly devalued the investment and caused BG Group to suffer significant losses. They also passed legislation that would make foreign investor access to Argentine courts more difficult. As a result, BG Group filed for arbitration under the terms of the treaty. But according to Argentina, their filing was premature.

Article 8 of the treaty, the dispute resolution clause, requires that an aggrieved investor first make recourse to the local courts of Argentina, giving the local judiciary up to 18 months to resolve the dispute before proceeding to arbitration. BG Group did not believe that they would receive reasonable treatment in the Argentine courts and thus skipped that part of Article 8 and went straight to arbitration at the International Center for the Settlement of Investment Disputes (ICSID) at the World Bank, which resolves most investor–state disputes under these treaties.

The first question presented to the arbitral panel was whether they had jurisdiction to hear the case at all, given the local litigation clause found in Article 8 of the treaty. The panel concluded that they did have jurisdiction due to the barriers Argentina erected against investor litigation in Argentine courts, which excused BG Group's failure to rely on those courts as stipulated in Article 8. On the merits of the case, the panel found that Argentina did not expropriate BG Group's investment; however, Argentina failed to provide fair and equitable treatment to BG Group. The panel awarded damages to BG Group.

Both parties appealed to the federal district court, which is the first level trial court in the U.S. federal system. BG Group appealed to the court to have their damage award enforced under the terms of the New York Convention. Argentina appealed to have the award vacated under the argument that the arbitrators lacked jurisdiction to hear the case at all. The district court agreed with BG Group and enforced the award.

Argentina appealed again, this time to the Court of Appeals for the District of Columbia Circuit. That court reversed the district court's decision, deciding that the court had the ability to review the case *de novo*—without deference to the arbitrators' decision. Doing so, the appellate court concluded that the arbitrators lacked jurisdiction to hear the case in the first instance and that BG Group was obligated under the terms of the treaty to litigate in Argentine courts for 18 months.

This time, BG Group appealed the decision, and the only court left to raise such an appeal to was the U.S. Supreme Court, which agreed to hear the case in June 2013. The court issued its decision in March 2014, nine months after initially agreeing to hear the case. The briefs exemplifying the logic of the parties are explained below.

BG Group's Argument

BG Group's argument was more challenging from the start because they were appealing a decision that reversed the authority of the arbitrators to hear their case at all and would ultimately send them back to Argentina to argue their case. The Court of Appeals had made a plain meaning interpretation of Article 8, finding that it left room for "skipping" the litigation process in Argentina and that this was undoubtedly a precondition to arbitration. Accordingly, for BG Group, this was a very difficult case to win.

The lawyers for BG Group knew that they could not win by arguing that they had the right to skip the litigation process outlined in the BIT. But they also knew that Argentina went along with the arbitration and that the arbitrators made a preliminary conclusion that they were empowered to decide the case even though Article 8 was violated. This opened a new line of argument for BG Group, one that considered the power of arbitrators rather than breach of a treaty provision.

Preliminary Arguments

BG Group began its argument with a summary of the key elements. First, arbitration is essential to international business and should be respected by the courts. Second, precedent establishes that courts have limited power to question arbitral decisions. Third, international legal principles agreed to by the parties confirm the ability of arbitrators to decide their own competence. And finally, regardless of the competence of the arbitral panel, Argentina blocked access to its courts, thereby making arbitration the only reasonable dispute resolution option.

In making their first point, BG Group asserted the importance of arbitration in international commercial disputes:

Arbitration constitutes "an almost indispensable precondition to achievement of the orderliness and predictability essential to any international business transaction."[7]

Then BG Group diminishes the role of the courts under Article 8, suggesting that even if they were utilized in a dispute like this, the parties would still have the ability to override that decision by going to arbitration:

> *Under Article 8, if a dispute regarding an investment arises between an investor and a contracting state, either party may submit it to "the competent tribunal" (i.e., the courts) of the contracting state. Id. art. 8(1), App. 8a-9a. But the judiciary has no power to render a final decision on the dispute. Instead, if either party remains dissatisfied after eighteen months in litigation—whether or not the local court has rendered a decision—the dispute "shall be submitted to international arbitration. . . . " Id. art. 8(2), App. 9a.*[8]

Having concluded that arbitration is sacrosanct and that litigation in Argentina is unnecessary because the arbitrators have the final say, BG Group moved on to emphasize the power of the arbitral panel to decide their own jurisdiction:

> *The Treaty provides that the arbitration presumptively will be conducted under the rules of the United Nations Commission on International Trade Law (UNCITRAL). Id. art. 8(3), App. 9a-10a. Article 21 of the UNCITRAL Rules grants the arbitral tribunal the power to "rule on objections that it has no jurisdiction." Rep. of the U.N. Comm. on Int'l Trade Law, 9th Sess., Apr. 12-May 7, 1976, U.N. Doc. A/31/17, at 24, art. 21(1); GAOR, 31st Sess., Supp. No. 17 (1976).*[9]

Driving the last nail in the coffin on the Argentine courts, BG Group asserts that the arbitral panel is not obligated to defer or even reference decisions of local courts in making its determinations. Likewise, local courts have no ability to review the decision of the arbitral panel.

Finally, BG Group focused on the efforts by Argentina to prevent BG Group a fair opportunity to resolve the dispute in local courts, including a decree staying all actions against the state for expropriation.[10] Here, they were laying the framework for their key argument that Argentina not only blocked BG Group from reasonable access to local courts, but that Argentina itself conceded to the use of arbitration to resolve the dispute.

First, the barriers to local court access:

> *BG alleged that by dismantling the regulatory framework that induced its investment—including by curtailing access to judicial redress—Argentina: (1) breached Article 5 of the Treaty by expropriating the value of BG's shareholding in its consortium and in MetroGAS, and by impairing BG's rights under the MetroGAS license; and (2) breached Article 2(2) of the Treaty by failing to provide BG with fair and equitable treatment, protection, and security, by taking unreasonable and discriminatory measures, by failing to observe obligations entered into with regard to BG's investments, and for the acts of its judiciary.*[11]

BG Group even went so far as to say that Argentina had the option of filing in its own courts, but it chose not to:

> *Argentina was entitled to respond by submitting the dispute to its own courts, see Treaty art. 8(1), App. 8a-9a, but it chose not to do so. Because the parties did not agree on a different arbitral system, the dispute was submitted to UNCITRAL arbitration.*[12]

Following this high-level summary, BG Group hones in on its two principal arguments: 1) Argentina consented to arbitration and 2) courts lack jurisdiction to overturn an arbitral determination of competence. I have highlighted some key aspects of their arguments in the following paragraphs.

Argentina Clearly Consented to Arbitrate

The first element of BG Group's argument attempts to declare a non-conflict. If Argentina consented to the arbitration and agreed that the panel could determine its own competence to hear the case, there is no reason for the court to be involved.

To emphasize their point here, BG Group alleged that not only did Argentina not attend the arbitration in protest, but it also was actively engaged in the four-year process:

> *Argentina participated actively in the arbitration. Particularly relevant here, Argentina expressly invoked and relied upon Article 21 of the UNCITRAL Rules—which gives the tribunal the power to determine its own jurisdiction—in requesting that the arbitrators enter an order dismissing BG's claim for lack of jurisdiction. Argentina argued, inter alia, that under the terms of the Treaty, BG could initiate arbitration only after eighteen months of litigation in an Argentine court.*[13]

Predicting that Argentina would again argue that the panel lacked jurisdiction, BG Group drew the court's attention to the in-depth analysis that the panel went through in determining whether it had jurisdiction over the parties. The panel concluded that:

> *As a matter of treaty interpretation, however, Article 8(2)(a)(i) cannot be construed as an absolute impediment to arbitration. Where recourse to the domestic judiciary is unilaterally prevented or hindered by the host State, any such interpretation would lead to the kind of absurd and unreasonable result proscribed by Article 32 of the Vienna Convention, allowing the state to unilaterally elude arbitration, which has been the engine of the transition from a politicized system of diplomatic protection to one of direct investor- State adjudication.*[14]
>
> . . .
>
> *a serious problem would loom if admissibility of Claimant's claims were denied thus allowing Respondent at the same time to: a) restrict the effectiveness of domestic judicial remedies as a means to achieve the full implementation of the Emergency Law and its regulations; b) insist that the Claimant go to domestic courts to challenge the very same measures; and c) exclude from the renegotiation process any licensee that does bring its grievance to local courts.*[15]

Arguing by analogy, BG Group identified two Second Circuit cases that, though the facts differed significantly, both addressed the threshold question of whether a party consents to arbitration. In each case, the court concluded that because the parties consented to the rules of UNCITRAL, they consented to have issues of arbitral validity addressed by the arbitral panel and not the courts.[16] Because Argentina also agreed to be bound by UNCITRAL rules, BG Group urged the court to align itself with this line of thinking.

BG Group suggested that Argentina recognized at the outset the competence of the arbitral panel to resolve competence issues. "Argentina affirmatively conceded that '[i]t is a well known principle that arbitral tribunals have the competence to determine their own competence.'"[17]

Courts Must Respect the Sanctity of Arbitration or the Entire System May Fail

The second argument pursued by BG Group is that by ruling in favor of Argentina, the Court would be substantially weakening the international commercial arbitration system and undermining the long-standing principles of the New York Convention on the Enforcement of International Arbitral Awards. Referring again to the *Scherk* case mentioned above, BG Group asserted:

> *A parochial refusal by the courts of one country to enforce an international arbitration agreement would not only frustrate these purposes, but would invite unseemly and mutually destructive jockeying by the parties to secure tactical litigation advantages.*[18]

Anticipating the counter-argument from Argentina, BG Group recognized the narrow grounds under which a court may override the arbitral decision. These grounds include fraud and corruption, as noted in the Federal Arbitration Act. But they also include "gateway" issues, which address the power of the arbitrators to hear the case at all, certainly an argument that Argentina would make. The exception comes from a 2002 Supreme Court case in which a securities dealer sued an investor for misrepresentation. The arbitration rules that the parties had agreed upon included a time bar for certain claims. The question there was who had the authority to determine whether the time bar had been exceeded—the courts or the arbitral panel itself.

> *deference to the arbitrators is not necessarily warranted when a challenge to the arbitrators' jurisdiction poses a substantive "question of arbitrability" concerning "the kind of narrow circumstance where contracting parties would likely have expected a court to have decided the gateway matter."*[19]

The Court deflected the time-bar question to the arbitrators in that case. They held that "gateway" issues that courts do have the authority to resolve include whether the parties agreed to arbitrate at all and whether an arbitration clause applies to a given subject matter. That was not present in the *Howsam* case nor is it present, argued BG Group, in BG Group's case with Argentina.

> *Argentina's jurisdictional objection is also inextricable from the merits of BG's arbitration claim, including BG's challenge to the very measures that obstructed its access to the Argentine courts.*
>
> *The court of appeals believed that the U.S. courts had primary decisional competence over all arbitrability questions under the Treaty. That view is misguided. No provision of the Treaty anticipates any role for the courts of the nation that hosts the arbitration (here, the United States). Even the Argentine courts have no power to decide anything finally. The Treaty grants the arbitral tribunal alone the power to issue a "final and binding" ruling. Any other rule would have defied common sense and would have erected a significant barrier to the very foreign investment that the Treaty was adopted to encourage. Investors will not risk hundreds of millions of dollars in investment unless they are sure that disputes will be resolved by a neutral and expert tribunal, not the local judicial arm of its government opponent.*[20]

The Treaty grants the arbitral tribunal alone the power to issue a "final and binding" ruling. Any other rule would have defied common sense and would have erected a significant barrier to the very foreign investment that the Treaty was adopted to encourage. Investors will not risk hundreds of millions of dollars in investment unless they are sure that disputes will be resolved by a neutral and expert tribunal, not the local judicial arm of its government opponent.[21]

Continuing on in this line of reasoning, BG Group asserted that the courts have very narrow power to review arbitral decisions unless they affect these gateway issues:

The "narrow circumstance[s]" presenting a question of substantive arbitrability, presumptively resolved by a court, include whether a party is bound at all by a particular arbitration clause and whether an arbitration clause applies to a particular type of controversy. Id. at 84. By contrast, "issues of procedural arbitrability, i.e., whether prerequisites such as time limits, notice, laches, estoppel, and other conditions precedent to an obligation to arbitrate have been met, are for the arbitrators to decide." Id. at 85 (emphasis altered) (quoting Revised Uniform Arbitration Act § 6(c), cmt. 2, 7 U.L.A. 12–13 (Supp. 2002)). This division of responsibility reflected "the kind of narrow circumstance where contracting parties would likely have expected a court to have decided the gateway matter," so that "reference of the gateway dispute to the court avoids the risk of forcing parties to arbitrate a matter that they may well not have agreed to arbitrate."[22]

BG Group then employed the tactic of arguing by analogy to make their point. They cited *Wiley v. Livingston*, which involved the preservation of union rights in a contract when that company merges with another entity. Though the facts were quite distinct, the question in that case was the same as this element in the BG Group case—when can a court dictate the terms of an arbitration.

[A]rbitrators should presumptively decide "whether the first two steps of a grievance procedure were completed, where these steps are prerequisites to arbitration." 537 U.S. at 84. In John Wiley, the agreement between an employer and a union included two preconditions to arbitration: the parties had to hold a conference among the affected employee, a union steward, and the employer or an officer of the employer; and then hold a second conference between an officer of the employer and a representative of the union. 376 U.S. at 555–56. Arbitration was permitted only "in the event that the grievance shall not have been resolved or settled" in one of those two steps. Id. at 556. After the agreement between the employer and the union was signed, an unforeseen event occurred: the employer was absorbed in a merger, and the newly merged entity denied that it was bound by the agreement (which the union disputed).[23]

The grievance procedure was a prerequisite to arbitration, but the court left it to the arbitral panel to decide whether that prerequisite had been complied with (or waived) by the parties. BG Group would have liked the court to do the same here—leave the procedural determinations to the arbitral panel.

Taking these two cases in tandem, BG Group argued that the court is obligated to overturn the lower court's ruling that the court has the power to determine whether preconditions to arbitration have been met:

This Court's precedent is therefore clear: absent clear and convincing evidence of a contrary agreement, a dispute concerning compliance with a precondition to arbitration must be decided by the arbitrators.[24]

Further sounding the alarm, BG Group referenced language from the Council for International Business to suggest that a decision in favor of Argentina would seriously damage the international investment environment:

If Argentina's position were to prevail, dissatisfied parties will have a new way to challenge in court otherwise fair and final arbitrations by arguing that preconditions to arbitration were not satisfied. This "would result in wasteful duplication, unnecessary use of judicial resources, and significant delay." . . . When, as here, the applicability of preconditions overlaps with the merits of the dispute, the decision would "open the door to the full-bore legal and evidentiary appeals that can rende[r] informal arbitration merely a prelude to a more cumbersome and time-consuming judicial review process, and bring arbitration theory to grief in postarbitration process." . . . In all likelihood, parties will not risk the inefficiency and unpredictability of a rule permitting courts to second-guess arbitral tribunals. Thus, investors will simply stop agreeing to site arbitrations in the United States. Ultimately, the nation's standing in the international business community would suffer.[25]

Argentina, the Bad Apple

In the event that the substantive legal arguments were unpersuasive, BG Group decided to get more personal and argue that Argentina has a history of bypassing court and arbitral judgments that it disagrees with. This argument has less legal persuasion than the jurisdictional argument, but it may tip the scales for justices who are uncertain of which way they will rule.

Each time domestic courts adopt rules that permit judicial second-guessing of arbitral awards, they encourage obstreperous parties—none of whom is more infamous than Argentina—to launch collateral litigation. The result not only undermines the orderly functioning of the arbitral system, but raises substantial doubts concerning the efficacy of the entire arbitral regime.[26]

To take their allegations about Argentina's non-compliance with legal decisions against it, BG Group cites to a *Wall Street Journal* article and argues:

This Court should approach warily Argentina's attempt to overturn the international arbitration award in BG's favor. Argentina is infamous for its history of agreeing to arbitrate international

> *commercial disputes, then contesting adverse arbitral awards by every possible judicial means, and then if it still loses, simply refusing to abide by the rulings of the courts to which it submitted the case—particularly, rulings of the American federal courts. "Argentina's strategy can be 'to use all means available to obstruct and delay the arbitration proceedings,' which could exhaust the plaintiff's patience and ward off other potential claimants from bringing cases."*[27]

"Argentina's general disdain for the U.S. judiciary is legendary."[28] "This Court should not encourage Argentina—and other litigants that might consider following its abusive model—by announcing a legal rule that undermines the authority of the parties' chosen arbitral tribunal."[29]

Notice how BG Group drew on secondary sources to bolster its policy argument that Argentina has a history of non-compliance with its obligations, making resort to its courts prior to going to arbitration effectively useless as a remedy. Their argument is further strengthened by suggesting that Argentina disrespects the U.S. judicial system, justifying the selection of arbitration as the exclusive remedy for dispute resolution. Their approach was successful in convincing the justices that the investment treaty's provision establishing a "local litigation" requirement was a procedural provision that could be evaluated by the arbitrators.

The court concluded that the local litigation requirement was merely a procedural provision and that, like any other contract, compliance with a procedural provision prior to arbitration is determined by the arbitrators, not the court. "Construing the local litigation provision as an 'absolute' requirement would mean Argentina could avoid arbitration by, say, passing a law that closed down its court system indefinitely or that prohibited investors from using its courts. Such an interpretation runs contrary to a basic objective of the investment treaty."[30]

What we learn from this case is not just that treaties are no different than contracts for purposes of interpretation, but also that even a provision that appears clear on its face can be overcome with effective argument. The language of the treaty in this case was relatively straightforward:

Arbitration is permitted: "(i) where, after a period of eighteen months has elapsed from the moment when the dispute was submitted to the competent tribunal . . . the said tribunal has not given its final decision; [or] (ii) where the final decision of the aforementioned tribunal has been made but the Parties are still in dispute."[31] From the plain reading of this clause, there appears to be no room to interpret this to mean that the parties can bypass the tribunal altogether. Yet that is precisely what BG Group did and what the court ultimately permitted.

The crux of Argentina's argument was that the treaty language obligated the parties to go to Argentina courts first, before even attempting arbitration. It has the language of the agreement on its side. However, BG Group had one big advantage on their side—they already went to arbitration and Argentina went along. These actions placed the determination of compliance with the terms of the treaty in the hands of the arbitrators and effectively silenced Argentina's only clear argument. From that point, BG Group only had to argue that threshold issues, such as compliance with preconditions to arbitration, were to be determined by the arbitrators, not the court. And they did just that.

Notes

1 Ruggero J. Aldisert, et al., *Logic for Law Students: How to Think Like a Lawyer*, 69 U. Pitt. L. Rev. 1 (2007) at 116, citing Edward Levi, *An Introduction to Legal Reasoning* 1–2 (1948).

2 *Adams v. New Jersey Steamboat Co.*, 45 N.E. 369 (N.Y. 1896).

3 *BG Group PLC v. Republic of Argentina*, No. 12-138 (2012), Brief for the Petitioner at page i, http://sblog.s3.amazonaws.com/wp-content/uploads/2012/10/12-138-BG-Cert-Reply-final.pdf.

4 *BG Group PLC v. Republic of Argentina*, No. 12-138 (2012), Brief for the Respondent at page i, http://sblog.s3.amazonaws.com/wp-content/uploads/2012/10/12-138-Brief-in-Opposition-filed-10-1-12.pdf.pdf.

5 Agreement for the Promotion and Protection of Investments, Art. 8(2), Dec. 11, 1990, 1765 U.N.T.S. 38, Art. 2(2), App. 4a.

6 Id., Arts 8(1), 8(2)(a)(i).

7 BG Group brief at 7, quoting *Scherk v. Alberto-Culver Co.*, 417 U.S. 506, 516 (1974).

8 BG Group brief at 7.

9 BG Group brief at 7.
10 BG Group brief at 10–11.
11 BG Group brief at 11.
12 BG Group brief at 11.
13 BG Group brief at 12.
14 BG Group brief at 13.
15 BG Group brief at 14.
16 BG Group brief at 51.
17 BG Group brief at 57.
18 *Scherk*, 417 U.S. at 516–517.
19 BG Group brief at 18, quoting *Howsam v. Dean Witter Reynolds, Inc.*, 537 U.S. 79, 83 (2002).
20 BG Group brief at 25–26.
21 BG Group brief at 26.
22 BG Group brief at 33.
23 BG Group brief at 34, citing *John Wiley and Sons, Inc. v. Livingston*, 376 U.S. 543 (1964).
24 BG Group brief at 35.
25 BG Group brief at 46.
26 BG Group brief at 26–27.
27 BG Group brief at 28, quoting Matt Moffett, *Besting Argentina in Court Doesn't Seem To Pay*, Wall St. J. (Apr. 20, 2012), http://online.wsj.com/article/SB10001424052702303425504577356262654410468.html.
28 BG Group brief at 29.
29 BG Group brief at 30–31.
30 *BG Group PLC v. Republic of Argentina*, 134 S. Ct. 1198, 1212 (2014) at 18.
31 Agreement for the Promotion and Protection of Investments, Arts. 8(1), (2)(a).

6

CONCLUDING REMARKS

Inside the Mind of the American Lawyer

The foundations of law that informed the development of the civil and common law systems are identical. Yet how we analyze, interpret, and ultimately argue about that law is fundamentally different. As an adversarial system based upon the principle of *stare decisis*, the American legal system has evolved into a highly sensitive and often very creative race to establish a beneficial outcome for a particular client. What results from these cases is an evolving common law that constantly adapts to the unique arguments of attorneys, who have little interest in creating predictable law but substantial interest in winning their cases.

In the common law, "[e]very new case is an experiment . . . The principles themselves are continually retested; for if the rules derived from a principle do not work well, the principle itself must ultimately be reexamined."[1]

This is a book about common law legal reasoning. Ordinarily, it might be reasonable to assume that everyone looks at law in a similar way—we read and apply a statute or case precedent in the same manner in a variety of cases. Yet much to the surprise and dismay of many law students and practitioners not trained in the ways of the common law, there is a great deal of unique interpretation that feeds the development of law in the United States and similar common law jurisdictions. Legal reasoning is the pathway through which law is understood.

No two lawyers look at a single case in precisely the same manner. Nor are they expected to. A common law lawyer has been trained to look beyond the superficial language and to dig into the meaning behind the words. Often applying his or her own wealth of experience and background in a certain area of law, each lawyer will find different value in the case, even if multiple lawyers are working for the same client.

Of course, in some cases, a single precedent or statute will be found that is hard to dispute on its face. This can be immensely helpful or terribly harmful, depending on the application of that precedent or statute. Yet even with this substantively aligned piece of law, the legal research and analysis process has only just begun. Much like the flour, the most substantial ingredient in baking a cake, is hardly noticeable once other ingredients have been added, common law researchers will shape their own arguments in the direction they wish through the use of many cases and statutes.

Take the following case excerpt as an example. Read the factual summary and applicable law and consider what you believe to be the most reasonable outcome:

The Religious Freedom Restoration Act of 1993 (RFRA) prohibits the "Government [from] substantially burden[ing] a person's exercise of religion even if the burden results from a rule of general applicability" unless the Government "demonstrates that application of the burden to the person—(1) is in furtherance of a compelling governmental interest; and (2) is the least restrictive means of furthering that compelling governmental interest." 42 U. S. C. §§2000bb–1(a), (b). As amended by the Religious Land Use and Institutionalized Persons Act of 2000 (RLUIPA), RFRA covers "any exercise of religion, whether or not compelled by, or central to, a system of religious belief." §2000cc–5(7)(A).

At issue here are regulations promulgated by the Department of Health and Human Services (HHS) under the Patient Protection and Affordable Care Act of 2010 (ACA), which, as relevant here, requires specified employers' group health plans to furnish "preventive care and screenings" for women without "any cost sharing requirements," 42 U. S. C. §300gg–13(a)(4). Congress did not specify what types of preventive care must be covered; it authorized the Health Resources and Services Administration, a component of HHS, to decide. Ibid. Nonexempt employers are generally required to provide coverage for the 20 contraceptive methods approved by the Food and Drug Administration, including the 4 that may have the effect of preventing an already fertilized egg from developing any further by inhibiting its attachment to the uterus. Religious employers, such as churches, are exempt from this contraceptive mandate. HHS has also effectively exempted religious nonprofit organizations with religious objections to providing coverage for contraceptive services. Under this accommodation, the insurance issuer must exclude contraceptive coverage from the employer's plan and provide plan participants with separate payments for contraceptive services without imposing any cost-sharing requirements on the employer, its insurance plan, or its employee beneficiaries.

In these cases, the owners of three closely held for-profit corporations have sincere Christian beliefs that life begins at conception and that it would violate their religion to facilitate access to contraceptive drugs or devices that operate after that point. In separate actions, they sued HHS and other federal officials and agencies (collectively HHS) under RFRA and the Free Exercise Clause, seeking to enjoin application of the contraceptive mandate insofar as it requires them to provide health coverage for the four objectionable contraceptives. In No. 13–356, the District Court denied the Hahns and their company—Conestoga Wood Specialties—a preliminary injunction. Affirming, the Third Circuit held that a for-profit corporation could not "engage in religious exercise" under RFRA or the First Amendment, and that the mandate imposed no requirements on the Hahns in their personal capacity. In No. 13–354, the Greens, their children, and their companies—Hobby Lobby Stores and Mardel—were also denied a preliminary injunction, but the Tenth Circuit reversed. It held that the Greens' businesses are "persons" under RFRA, and that the corporations had established a likelihood of success on their RFRA claim because the contraceptive mandate substantially burdened their exercise of religion and HHS had not demonstrated a compelling interest in enforcing the

> *mandate against them; in the alternative, the court held that HHS had not proved that the mandate was the "least restrictive means" of furthering a compelling governmental interest.*[2]

So the basic question in this case is whether the statute referenced in the first paragraph, the Religious Freedom Restoration Act of 1993 (RFRA), applies to corporations. If it does, it would mean that a corporation is allowed to use the Act to opt-out of certain elements of health coverage under the Affordable Care Act—namely, contraceptives. Now that you are familiar with the facts and legal issue, how might you answer these questions:

1. Corporations are considered "people" by law in many instances, such as for purposes of taxation and criminality. What about with respect to the freedom of religion?
2. Corporations are legal entities that are designed by and controlled by people. Do those people (shareholders) have the ability to effectuate their own religious beliefs *through* the corporation?

These are two of the big questions that the Court struggled with. The majority sided with the corporation and found a clear right for the corporation to seek protection of its First Amendment freedom of religion rights under the Act. Here is how they answered the two questions I posed above:

> *RFRA's text shows that Congress designed the statute to provide very broad protection for religious liberty and did not intend to put merchants to such a choice. It employed the familiar legal fiction of including corporations within RFRA's definition of "persons," but the purpose of extending rights to corporations is to protect the rights of people associated with the corporation, including shareholders, officers, and employees. Protecting the free-exercise rights of closely held corporations thus protects the religious liberty of the humans who own and control them. Pp. 16–19.*

And to the second question:

> *Any suggestion that for-profit corporations are incapable of exercising religion because their purpose is simply to make money flies in the face of modern corporate law. States, including those in which the plaintiff corporations were incorporated, authorize corporations to pursue any lawful purpose or business, including the pursuit of profit in conformity with the owners' religious principles. Pp. 20–25.*

So the logic of the majority here was that . . .

> *The means the Government chose is the imposition of a direct mandate on the employers in these cases. But in other instances the Government has allowed the same contraception coverage in issue here to be provided to employees of nonprofit religious organizations, as an accommodation to the religious objections of those entities. (CONCURRENCE)*

What were the considerations that the court relied upon to reach its decision that corporations may take advantage of the freedom of religion provision within the First Amendment? The main contention appears to be that, as a legal person, a corporation should be able to enjoy most, if not all, of the same rights as a natural person. The argument that a corporation exists in the law only as a vehicle to earn profit for its owners was dismissed by the court because a corporation can come into legal existence for many purposes, including ones not associated with earning a profit.

Our legal system, like many others, has long recognized that corporations are legal persons for certain purposes:

> *Under the designation of "person" there is no doubt that a private corporation is included. Such corporations are merely associations of individuals united for a special purpose and permitted to do business under a particular name and have a succession of members*

> *without dissolution. As said by Chief Justice Marshall: "The great object of a corporation is to bestow the character and properties of individuality on a collective and changing body of men." Providence Bank v. Billings, 4 Pet. 514, 29 U.S. 562.*[3]

But this did not initially imply that they enjoy *all* the rights that natural persons enjoy. In early cases, they were not permitted to the privileges and immunities clause of the Constitution, which states: "the citizens of each state shall be entitled to all privileges and immunities of citizens in the several states."[4]

This clause protects the fundamental rights of citizens across all states. When citizens move between states, they cannot be denied these fundamental rights. However, this has not been expanded to protect commercial activity:

> *[C]orporations are not citizens within the meaning of the [privileges and immunities] clause; that the term "citizens," as used in the clause, applies only to natural persons, members of the body politic owing allegiance to the state, not to artificial persons created by the legislature, and possessing only such attributes as the legislature has prescribed; that the privileges and immunities secured to citizens of each state in the several states by the clause in question are those privileges and immunities which are common to the citizens in the latter states, under their Constitution and laws, by virtue of their citizenship; that special privileges enjoyed by citizens in their own states are not secured in other states by that provision; that it was not intended that the laws of one state should thereby have any operation in other states; that they can have such operation only by the permission, express or implied, of those states; that special privileges which are conferred must be enjoyed at home unless the assent of other states to their enjoyment therein be given, and that a grant of corporate existence was a grant of special privileges to the corporators, enabling them to act for certain specified purposes as a single*

> *individual, and exempting them, unless otherwise provided, from individual liability, which could therefore be enjoyed in other states only by their assent.*[5]

In the preceding case, the issue was whether a closely held family run corporation could seek an exemption from the requirements under federal law to provide insurance coverage for their employees, which includes coverage for contraceptives. The company is run by a religious family that does not want to provide support, however indirect, for the purchase of birth control because of their religion. "[T]he owners of three closely held for-profit corporations have sincere Christian beliefs that life begins at conception and that it would violate their religion to facilitate access to contraceptive drugs or devices that operate after that point."[6]

The individual owners of the corporation have a clear right to object to the funding of contraceptives on the basis of their religion. In addition, religious organizations such as churches are also exempt from the requirement to provide coverage for contraceptives. However, this case asks whether the right of individuals to object to such coverage transfers from the owners to the corporation as a separate legal entity.

The court agreed with the petitioners (Hobby Lobby) that their beliefs could be associated with the corporation and that a corporation that "holds" such beliefs could object on religious grounds to the coverage requirement. The court was clear, however, that the ability of a corporation to object on religious grounds applied only to closely held corporations, not to all corporations.

What we learn from this case is that a single party, in this case a chain of hobby stores, can have a significant effect on a law that will ultimately apply to thousands of other similarly situated individuals or entities. The effect of legal reasoning on the entire legal system in the United States is substantial, and, what you can hopefully see by now, it is largely driven not by legislators or even judges, but by the attorneys that craft effective legal arguments.

As the representatives of individuals and businesses, attorneys use their training in critical thinking and logic to shape the very heart of our legal system—precedent.

As lawyers trained outside the U.S. engage more frequently and more substantively with the U.S. legal system, they will need to develop more refined legal analysis skills that will be effective in U.S. courts and arbitral bodies. Though the best preparation would be to study in a Juris Doctor program, which is case-intensive and hones your critical analysis skills for three years, my hope is that this book provided you with some of the tools necessary to embark on your career in cross-border legal analysis. To stay sharp, I recommend routinely reading U.S. court opinions, especially from the U.S. Supreme Court and the federal courts of appeal, to get accustomed to the use of inductive, deductive, and analogic analysis.

Notes

1 Munroe Smith, *Jurisprudence* 21 (1909).
2 *Burwell v. Hobby Lobby Stores, Inc.*, No. 13–354, 723 F. 3d 1114.
3 *Pembina Consolidated Silver Mining Co. v. Pennsylvania,* 125 U.S. 181 (1888) at 125.
4 U.S. Const. Art. IV, § 2.
5 *Pembina Consolidated Silver Mining Co.*, 125 U.S. at 124–125.
6 *Burwell v. Hobby Lobby Stores, Inc.*, 134 S. Ct. 2751, 2766 (2014), Syllabus.

INDEX

For Product Safety Concerns and Information please contact our EU
representative GPSR@taylorandfrancis.com
Taylor & Francis Verlag GmbH, Kaufingerstraße 24, 80331 München, Germany

www.ingramcontent.com/pod-product-compliance
Ingram Content Group UK Ltd.
Pitfield, Milton Keynes, MK11 3LW, UK
UKHW022121190926
475702UK00013B/1564
9780323356473